Return To Acts Christianity

The Reformation God & His People Are *Yearning* For –
Beyond the Walls of Traditional Church Structure

DAVID O'BRIEN

All For The Prize Publications

© 2010, 2012, 2015, 2017 by *David O'Brien*
ISBN: 978-0-9828843-5-5

All rights reserved. This book is protected by the copyright laws of the United States of America. This book may not be copied or reprinted for commercial gain or profit. The use of quotations or photocopying for personal or group study, or for free distribution without distorting the original work, is permitted and encouraged. Credit and contact information must be included as follows: "Return To Acts Christianity – The Reformation God & His People are Yearning for – Beyond the Walls of Traditional Church Structure," www.actschristianity.com, Copyright © 2017, Used by permission." Other permission may be granted upon request.

The excerpt by Derek Prince, used by permission, is taken from *Rediscovering God's Church* by Derek Prince. Copyright © 2006 by Derek Prince Ministries–International. Use by permission of Whitaker House. www.whitakerhouse.com.

Scripture quotations are taken from the following Bible versions:
The New King James Version. Copyright © 1982 by Thomas Nelson, Inc. Used by permission. All rights reserved.
The NEW AMERICAN STANDARD BIBLE®, Copyright © 1960,1962,1963,1968,1971,1972,1973,1975,1977, 1995 by The Lockman Foundation. Used by permission.
The HOLY BIBLE, NEW INTERNATIONAL VERSION®. Copyright © 1973, 1978, 1984 Biblica. Used by permission of Zondervan. All rights reserved.

Abbreviations are as follows:
NKJ – New King James Version
NASB – New American Standard Bible
NIV – New International Version

Previous editions were entitled, "Return," "Jesus' Original Church," and "Leadership Without Limits – Laying Down the Four Walls of Traditional Church Structure."

All For The Prize Publications
www.allfortheprize.com

www.actschristianity.com

Responses to *Return To Acts Christianity*

"*Return To Acts Christianity* should be read and studied by everyone who is seriously interested in pleasing our Lord when they are "doing church." I recommend it to all, from bishops of cathedrals, to "laymen" attempting to begin a house church. You need this!

Jesus is our pattern in living, in family, in community, and in all relationships, regardless of the context. Because "church" is about all of these, it is critical to know His full intentions. Christians often tend to set aside Jesus' wishes about it, thinking them odd, out of step with the times, or just too difficult. But after all, it is His Church, He is determined to be the Head, and we may not have much help from him, if we ignore His blueprints. His disciples recognized this, carefully tailoring the early church communities accordingly, and they gave us both a record and their specific definitions of the process and the problems included, in the New Testament.

David O'Brien has been very thorough and meticulous in helping us to understand something of great importance, something not often modeled in our day. You may not agree with all of his conclusions, but if God has made you responsible for some part of his Church, I highly recommend this book for your study.

I have been a church planter, an elder, a pastor, a missionary, and a student of the church in the Scriptures and in history for more than 50 years. I have seldom seen a book about Jesus' Church more carefully documented with the Scriptures. This book is not a novel; it is a serious manual, which requires some study. People who are committed to this most important kind of spiritual, but very human, community called "church" should read it soon!"

—Gary Henley, President & Executive Director of *International Outreach Ministries*, author of *The Quiet Revolution*

"David O'Brien's book on finding Jesus' Church is a light in the twilight over God's People. His voice is salient and powerful in the cry of the Spirit for the Church today. It is a cry for us to return to our first love."

—Evan Wiggs, a loving, powerful evangelist, author of *Engines of Heaven*

"This is one of the most impacting and educational books I've ever read for my spiritual growth. One of the big lessons I learned is that I need to follow Jesus, to walk into and carry out his plan for my life. Jesus is my shepherd. I belong to him and him alone. I should not allow my attachment to an organization interfere with my calling in Jesus Christ. I recommend this book to every sincere and hungry-for-truth Christian no matter how long you've been in Christianity. If you are a new believer, this book will help you start on a right track and give you a clear vision for your future walk. If you've been a Christian for a while, even decades, this book can cleanse you, refresh you and lead you to a new level of walking with God."

—Anonymous Chinese disciple

"This is an excellent addition to the many books written in recent years about GOD's design for His Church. I recommend it to all."

—Nate Krupp, house-meeting pioneer, author of *The Church Triumphant at the End of the Age* and *God's Simple Plan for His Church - and Your Place in It*

"David O'Brien has given us a wonderful tool. His book is concise and Biblically based. I pray that many leaders are able to get a copy."

—David Witt, CEO of *Spirit of Martyrdom Ministries*, Associate Rep. for *The Voice of the Martyrs*, co-author of *Fearless Love*

"David O'Brien has a heart after God. He is one of the new breed whose commitment is to bringing new wine into New Testament wineskins where the dynamic of the Holy Spirit works through all believers for ministry and evangelism. The insights in this book will challenge you, instruct you, excite you and probably upset you, but will not leave you the same. Herein lies a deep battle cry not to settle for sedentary forms that fail to empower every believer. May the Lion of Judah prevail!"

—Wayne Hayworth, disciple with over 40 years in Christianity, including leadership in traditional and non-traditional forms

For the Freedom, Unity, Development, and
Full Expression of God's
Royal People

Dedication

To those who have ears to hear this message. To those who are not content with the present state of the Church and the world. To those willing to step out of the way and let Jesus flow through them.

Special Thanks

First of all I want to thank the Lord Jesus, who thought of me and pulled me out of the garbage heap. He's the best teacher and shepherd there is. I thank you Jesus for mercy and patience and for encouraging and strengthening me to run the race with perseverance and hope. I offer this work up to you, my Lord and King.

I also want to thank my wife, for her precious support as I wrote this book. I thank God for the precious gift he's given me in her, such a special and wonderful person, the love of my life. Thank you for patience, prayer, encouragement, and editing. Your complement after editing the first draft was one of the greatest I've received in my life.

Thank you, also, to the many friends and others who helped me with this through editing, prayer, encouragement...

I want to publicly thank God for RC and Sheila Wedner. Much of what I've shared in this book I received through RC's fatherly mentoring years ago. To this day, they are great blessings to me, and I ask anyone blessed by this book to pray for and bless them. I hope this book makes you proud, RC.

RC and Sheila introduced me to two teachers that each greatly contributed to my growth and to this book: Dale Sides and Derek Prince. I thank God for both of these men who lowered themselves so Jesus could work through them. I haven't kept up with Dale's ministry since 2000 or Derek Prince Ministries since Derek left this earth. But for Dale and Derek Prince Ministries, I hope this book comes back around to be a blessing to you.

Foreword

It has been my God-given privilege to have been in David's path through life and I thank God for that. It's my observation that everybody develops some form of doctrine for life, some more than others. Doctrine is our rule for life and we have to have rules to keep order inside our very being. David has taken the more noble route and sought out the Creator of all things, the God and father of Jesus Christ. Looking deeply into his book, the Bible, and not following the traditions of our time, David has exposed truths that have been covered, without which Christians have been held back from the full life that God would have them to live. I am looking forward to the story about his life that will either be written by him or, for sure, by angels in Heaven.

We are all writing our own stories, and how we live will be based on the doctrine that we hold in our souls. That is why this book is a must read. I would challenge everyone young and old to consider what David has put forth here. It is not just David's, but the work of many men and what God has revealed to them in these, the last days of man's judgment. As we approach the Lord's Day and his judgment, we will need good strong doctrine to be able to stand victorious against the devil and his hosts. These are the proving hours, and more has been revealed than any time since the first century church. In this book, you can look and see many of these truths which have been brought together in one place. "You shall know the truth and the truth shall make you free." Write your own story of freedom and power, and live a full life. My blessings to all!

–RC Wedner

Table of Contents

Introduction   xii

Part 1: The Leadership Jesus Initiated
1. Historical Context   1
2. Jesus' Instruction for His Church Soon Before Its Birth   6
3. Further Teaching on Jesus' Church After He Left   11
4. More on Elders of God's Churches   15
5. Apostles & Elders Work Together   22
6. Holy vs. Unholy Ambition   26

Part 2: In Desperate Need of Reform
7. Indications of Our Present "Wretchedness"   29
8. Recent Revelation from God Regarding Reform   34
9. Why do Traditions of Men Go Down So Hard?   39
10. What Does God Really Require?   42
11. How Our Structure & Meeting Practice Changed   50

Part 3: Rediscovering the Basics
12. Jesus Has a Vision   54
13. What Does "Church" *Really* Mean?   61
14. Returning to the Simplicity & Power of Jesus' Legislature   67
15. Accountability Within The Legislature   75
16. The Distribution & Boundaries of God's Legislatures   78
17. Uses of Ekklesia in Scripture   84
18. The Unity of God's Legislatures   88

Part 4: The Five Equipping-Ministries *& Beyond Them*
19. Evangelism: the Way into the Legislature   95
20. Teachers, Prophets & Shepherding   105
21. Understanding the Work of Apostles   111
22. Restoring the Gift of Shepherds   118
23. The Two Highest Ministries   124
24. The Healing of Three Breaches   129
25. Re-centering Around Jesus Rather Than Individual Ministries   135

Part 5: Original Christian Activities
26. A Form That Holds The Spirit   139
27. Activity #1: Teaching   145
28. Activity #2: Fellowship   150
29. Activity #3: Financially Caring for Each Other   167
30. Activity #4: Prayer, Praise, & Other Priestly Offerings   171
31. Activity #5: Evangelism   178

32. The Result of the Combination of These Activities   184
33. Gifts in Every Legislature   186
34. Money Collection & Allocation   202

Part 6: Knowing All This, What do I do?
35. Submission is Necessary, Cleansing, & Powerful   204
36. We're Free to Serve Humbly in Love   209
37. Look up to Jesus   216
38. Questions & Answers   223
39. For Leadership without Limits   228
40. A Vision of Our Future (by Derek Prince)   232

I Have a (Christian) Dream   238

Epilogue: In View of Your Future Harvest   239

Bibliography & Recommended Resources   241

Introduction

It's time that the ceremonies of the Church of Jesus Christ on Earth are reformed.

In the period of the Reformation, Martin Luther and others began to reform the doctrine of the institutional church in Europe. Church doctrine was corrupted and truth hidden during the period known as the Dark Ages. This reform was monumental and we're receiving great benefits of it today. However, the fundamental structure of the church—also corrupted through the Dark Ages—was not reformed, at least not much. This study is to help us do so.

By way of introduction, this book is written out of love and genuine concern for believers, not out of bitterness. It's not (NOT) meant to produce bitterness, pride, or a revolutionary attitude in its readers. I have to include negatives, but my heart is to bring positives to light through this book. As believers we're not allowed to grumble or complain about anything. We should intercede. I am writing this book because these truths have been growing in me for many years, and I know it's now time to birth them.

Many people have been used of God to serve me with much of what you'll read here and to bless my life. I thank God for them! This book is for "faithful people who will also be qualified to, in turn, teach others" (2Tim 2:2).

Toward that end, I recommend you read this book with an open and teachable heart in order to receive seeds of truth from the Lord through it. As recorded in the Parable of the Farmer, once Jesus sows his precious seeds in you, your responsibility is to keep them within "an honest and good heart"—through meditation of them to sink down roots, through a wise lifestyle so the truths are not choked by the weeds, and through perseverance—and in the end, you will bear fruit through them (Lk 8:4-18).

Part 1: The Leadership Jesus Initiated

Chapter 1
Historical Context

The following is generally understood regarding Christian history. The Gospel began to be spoken by the Lord himself on Earth. Previously, it was spoken of and foreshadowed in the Old Testament as well. Then after Jesus ascended, we entered the time period of "The Great Mystery," which we're still in, and Jesus began to reveal the Great Mystery to us openly, through apostles and prophets such as Paul, Peter, Barnabas and many others (Eph 3:4-5).

Before Jesus left the earth he gave "The Great Commission," which included both evangelism (Mk 16) and caring for the souls of believers through discipleship (Mt 28). Jesus' early followers obeyed him, often to the death, and the Gospel was preached to every person in several parts of the Middle East, Asia, and Europe. Thomas took it as far as the southern part of India, according to history. It likely reached into China, as witnessed by the Chinese writing system, largely formed around the same time and which contains some Gospel truths in them by pictograph. The Gospel was extended to Africa, where discipleship began with the Ethiopian eunuch, as we see in the book of Acts. It is also reported that Mark helped take the Gospel to Egypt, at the cost of his physical life.[1]

When Jesus shed all his blood out on the cross, he ended Satan's ages-old reign. In Colossians, Paul says Jesus stripped

---

[1] John Foxe, *Foxe's Christian Martyrs* (Barbour Publishing, 2010), 15.

Satan of his armor (Col 2:15). John says "the ruler of this world" was "cast out" (Jn 12:31). Jesus armed us with his own righteousness, embarrassed Satan, and left him defenseless. Then Jesus sent his disciples out to gather the spoil (Jn 12:32). As they went, the enemy tried to fight by witchcraft and governmental persecution, but the believers overcame all that. The unbelievers "couldn't stand the wisdom" or the miracles of the believers (Ac 6:10). And the believers rejoiced when physically persecuted (Ac 5:41)! They saw martyrdom as a promotion, as in the case of Stephen. The sting of death had already been removed by Jesus' blood! Praise the Lord! They were unstoppable.

So the enemy tried to bring division into the new Church. In one case it was related to racial background (Grecian Jews verses Hebraic Jews, see Ac 6:1). But this turned into an opportunity for good, and a new ministry became known to God's People, "deacons." (Literal Greek: "attendants," "waiters," or "servers"). Other attempts at division were also squelched and turned for the further and more efficient advancement of the Kingdom of God through his People.

Because the work of Jesus on the cross was all-powerful, Satan had to somehow blind the Church to it, or distract us. He eventually used individuals who compromised in their own lives—they didn't want to face persecution from staunch unbelievers for the truth of the Gospel, and to justify their own compromise, they compromised the message as well (Rom 16:17-18, Gal 6:12).

These people wouldn't proclaim the cross. They taught the observance of the Law of Moses as the way to be made righteous, rather than the cross of the Messiah. Through their human influence and false doctrine, people started to get their eyes off of the cross (Gal 3:1). Their foundation for righteousness started to become some human observance they could do, such as circumcision (becoming a Jew) or observing feasts. By this, Paul said in Galatians that the believers there, who'd been saved by grace, through the cross, had come under a curse and had been bewitched (Gal 3:1). He tried to shift their focus back to the cross, the grace of God, and to walking by the

Spirit of God who gives us new Life through the new birth. Paul seems to have succeeded for a while in Galatia and Colossae. At any rate, this appears to be Paul's biggest battle. It wasn't from outside the Church as much as from inside.

Thank God that the opposition turned for an opportunity to establish doctrine for us today.

Satan has continued to attempt to obscure the cross—to blind us from it. All over the world, wherever God's People are found, Satan will try this. After Israel was dispersed into most all the nations of the world, Satan quit using his servants to obscure the cross primarily by teaching the observance of the Law of Moses to be saved, though he still will do this today when he can. Instead he had them create new, *human laws to divert attention from the cross*. These were traditions of men, and they can be seen in every region the Gospel went to. The doctrines vary but are similar in function.

However, this is not where the enemy stopped in his counterattack against us. He was terrified of the new Church, people with Christ in them—the same Christ who whooped him so badly in Israel, people who were commissioned by Christ to go into *every* nation and do the same works and even greater works than Jesus did. So, in order to inject these false doctrines and subtle distractions, which Jesus referred to as yeast, the devil sought to *plant his workers in the Church* and give them a voice. He wanted them to have a position of dominance so they could speak without interference. In Jesus parable, The Weeds Among the Wheat (Mt 13:24-30, 36-42), he foretold of this happening and called these implants, "sons of the Evil One." They operated by a counterfeit spirit—not the Holy Spirit. For this reason, John told believers to, "test the spirits to see if they're from God or not" (1Jn 4:1).

These three aspects of Satan's counterfeit of Christianity, a false message, false leaders, and false spirits, were his counterattack against the attack Jesus launched. They were all warned of by Paul in 2Corinthians 11:4. He spoke of "another Jesus," a "different spirit," and a "different gospel." The "another Jesus" has historically been in the form of a misrepresentation of the real Jesus (like Islam which said he didn't really die and wasn't the Son of God). Or it has been in the form of a minister who stands in the place of Jesus and gets the attention of God's People on him as if he is the head of the Church or a Church. Diotrephes was one of these who the apostle John had to deal with. John said, he "loves to be first among them" (3Jn vs. 9).

This kind of a person lifts himself up and takes dominion over people under him. He sees himself above them and crosses boundaries in their lives which he has no right to cross. Paul on the other hand said, "we preach not ourselves," and said of himself and his co-workers, "not that we have dominion over your faith, but we are *workers together with you*, for your joy" (2Cor 1:24).

The first apostles, trained by Jesus himself, were so free in the way they and the elders oversaw Churches that God could raise up a Paul who could seemingly go beyond their ability, and they gave him the right hand of fellowship. They kept the right Jesus, the right Gospel message, and the right Spirit.

It is obvious that there were some issues with James at a certain time, or at least with some people he sent (Gal 2:12). Peter also got off track temporarily (Gal 2:11). This just shows how hard it is to maintain these three important things even starting so well like they did.

Eventually the Roman Catholic Church-organization emerged. In other parts of the world, other very similar groups solidified as well. Examples include the Eastern Orthodox Church and the Coptic Christian Church of Egypt, also The Ethiopian Orthodox Church, and there are several others. In this book I will more specifically refer to the Roman Catholic one from time to time. I only do this because the Protestant church-organizations have many of their roots in it, and many of my readers will likely be from Protestant movements.

When Martin Luther challenged the authority of this huge organization, if it wasn't for God preserving him he would've been steamrolled by it. He challenged a lot of false doctrine and associated false practices of his day, and restored several things clearly revealed in Scripture.

Of course his restoration of doctrine wasn't complete. He

was followed by others who continued to restore truth: in the 1700s the idea of the Great Commission started to come back to God's People; in the 1800s travelling to teach and evangelize began to come back; in the early 1900s the power of the Spirit began to be restored; more recently, the idea of personal evangelism has come back, that all can evangelize, not just preachers appointed by denominations.[2]

There are several aspects of doctrine that are still being restored. Some have just barely begun to be restored. It's all in the Bible. The Spirit is leading us into all Truth. However, in this book I won't address many of the Gospel truths that are currently being restored. My goal here is to address the fundamental issues of Church identity, structure, and practice.

---

[2] T.L. Osborne, *Soul Winning* (OSFO Books International, 1994), 256-301.

Chapter 2
Jesus' Instruction for His Church Soon Before Its Birth

Jesus is the Chief Cornerstone of the Church. He said he would build his Church, and he began by personal example and instruction for his disciples.

Jesus' time with his disciples on Earth was training for them to bear the responsibility of going and evangelizing all the world and making disciples in every nation. Those who would believe would become his Church (we'll cover what this means in Chapter 13). They would become disciples and be taught everything Jesus taught the first disciples and more, as he would continue to teach his People after he rose from the dead (Jn 16:12-14). One thing Jesus commanded his disciples to teach those who believe was the Great Commission itself. In this way, when a disciple was trained, he too was to participate in this commission.

These first disciples would have to carry the message and the power to do all this. They would become "servants of the New Covenant," and to become adequate for such a task they needed to be trained:

Mark 2:21-22 (NKJ): No one sews a piece of unshrunk cloth on an old garment; or else the new piece pulls away from the old, and the tear is made worse. And no one puts new wine into old wineskins; or else the new wine bursts the wineskins, the wine is spilled, and the wineskins are

ruined. But new wine must be put into new wineskins.

The only wineskins fit to hold the power and glory and truth and grace of the New Covenant are the ones Jesus created by the training of his disciples.

Jesus contrasted the way religious leaders of his day acted with how he wanted the leaders of his Church to act:

Matt 23:5-12 (NKJ): …all their works they do to be seen by men. They make their phylacteries broad and enlarge the borders of their garments. They love the best places at feasts, the best seats in the synagogues, greetings in the marketplaces, and to be called by men, 'Rabbi, Rabbi.' But you, do not be called 'Rabbi'; for One is your Teacher, the Christ, and you are all brethren. Do not call [Gr., "your father(s) on earth"]; for One is your Father, He who is in heaven. And do not be called teachers; for One is your Teacher, the Christ. But he who is greatest among you shall be your servant.

Those in Jesus' Church, according to his Word here, are not to seek glory or exaltation in the eyes of men. Notice, the best place at a feast was not the problem, loving those places was. Receiving honor and acknowledgment when it's due is good (Ro 12:10, 13:7; Phil 2:29-30), but these leaders were loving it.

In that religious world, these people were taking on titles as an identity, for a place of superiority over those around them—not as a function. This is also forbidden. That's why he said, "you are all brothers." Our highest identity is sons and daughters of God, and we all share that status.

At one time, I thought the verse was saying to never identify people by their functions (E.g., "Pastor Rick," "Teacher Jack"). But it doesn't actually say that.

The equipping functions given in the New Testament, including "teacher" and "evangelist" (E.g., Eph 4:11, Ac 13:1, 1Tim 2:7, 2Tim 1:11) are job descriptions. They don't divide the Body but are given to uplift it. In the New Testament, these functions are named for identification purposes, to maintain awareness and expectation, and for order. We need to use them. We just need to also guard against misusing them.

About fathers, Jesus acknowledged first that we do have earthly fathers; then he said "you only have one father, the one in Heaven." Jesus was using *hyperbole* here, an exaggerated form of speaking for the sake of emphasis.

He used hyperbole elsewhere, e.g., "If anyone comes to Me, and does not hate his own father and mother and wife and children and brothers and sisters, yes, and even his own soul, he cannot be My disciple." (Luke 14:26). Someone who doesn't understand hyperbole could be confused here. He meant following him will require you to give up everyone around you and even the desires of your own soul.

When Jesus said, "Call none of your fathers on earth 'father,'" he was simply saying to see God as your father first and foremost. By understanding hyperbole, I don't believe he's meaning I'm to never call a father on earth, "dad" or "father." He means I must keep my focus primarily on my Father, God.

Some cultures within Christianity use titles in front of names; some use "brother/sister" before all names. There is no clear precedent for either in Scripture. John, one of Jesus' closest disciples, referred to himself as "the elder" in 3Jn vs. 1. Paul addressed, "King Agrippa" in Acts 26:19. Fathers were also addressed (e.g., Mt 15:4, Ac 7:2, Ro 4:16, 1Cor 4:15-17, 1Jn 2:13-14). Most modern groups say, "Evangelist Philip"; Acts 21:8 says, "Philip the evangelist." Is there any real difference?

I have my personal preference of how to address people, but when I go to a place and see how their culture is, I can stay flexible, honor the group's preferences, and serve within their system. Jesus does not want His Body divided over minor differences or disputable matters (Ro 14:1). We have freedom in these things, as long as we always lift everyone up.

Jesus revealed a totally new leadership style, not seen in the Gentile world, and ordained it as the way his Church was to be managed:

Matt 20:25-28 (NKJ): But Jesus called them to Himself

and said, "You know that the rulers of the Gentiles lord it over them, and those who are great exercise authority over them. Yet it shall not be so among you; but whoever desires to become great among you, let him be your servant. And whoever desires to be first among you, let him be your slave—just as the Son of Man did not come to be served, but to serve, and to give His life a ransom for many."

This verse contrasts how Jesus wants his leaders to approach his people and the way worldly leadership works. The two are 180 degrees different. Jesus' way is so opposite the thinking of fallen man that at the end of three years of training, Peter couldn't comprehend Jesus washing his feet. It still blows our minds today that Jesus stoops and washes our feet. He's our example.

Those who use the power of God more than others, do so not because they are greater and more exalted but because they've made a choice to be lowly servants of others, to put others above them.

Leadership from God gives the right to go first in being persecuted or taking heat for others. It gives room for servanthood. Paul and others followed this way. The Corinthian believers were being deceived by "super apostles" because they had a worldly view of leadership and prestige (2Cor 11:5). Paul emphasized his credentials and tried to straighten them out by revealing to them that he and the other true apostles were considered, "the scum of the earth," the lowest of all (1Cor 4:13). The choice the first apostles made to endure that gave them an honorable place in the New Jerusalem. Jesus gets to be lowest in it—as the foundation and cornerstone. They come next, under everyone else (Rev 21:14). Though Jesus is the highest exalted being, on the throne of God infinitely high, he is also the most humiliated of all, the slain lamb.

Spiritual leadership—the only kind Jesus approves of in his Church—works this way. The way up is down. He who humbles himself will be exalted. It's not how high we can go. It's how low we can go, given the opportunities God gives us. And it's not making a name for ourselves; it's "becoming of no reputation" (Phil 2:7). If we don't take that step in following Jesus, we won't be conformed fully to his image. This is why Jesus said that in the end, when he returned, "many who are first will be last and many last will be first" (Mt 19:30). Many in leadership positions who choose or accept a position of preeminence over their brothers today will be made last in the Kingdom when Jesus comes. It's absolutely scary to take a leadership position in Jesus' Church which operates in the way the world's leaders do.

Two more Scriptures before moving on:

Luke 20:45-47 (NKJ): Then, in the hearing of all the people, He said to His disciples, "Beware of the scribes, who desire to go around in long robes, love greetings in the marketplaces, the best seats in the synagogues, and the best places at feasts, who devour widows' houses, and for a pretense make long prayers. These will receive greater condemnation."

Luke 22:25-27 (NKJ): And He said to them, "The kings of the Gentiles exercise lordship over them, and those who exercise authority over them are called 'benefactors' ["philanthropists"]. But [it is] not [to be] so among you; on the contrary, he who is greatest among you, let him be as the younger, and he who governs as he who serves. For who is greater, he who sits at the table, or he who serves? Is it not he who sits at the table? Yet I am among you as the One who serves. "

Chapter 3
Further Teaching on Jesus' Church After He Left

After Jesus left, he continued to teach his disciples many things through the Spirit, as he had promised (Jn 16:12-14). Here are some of them:

- The Church is Jesus' Body. He's the Head. Nourishment for the whole body comes from him and through the connected parts. Direction also comes from the head in a body. It receives input from the body and makes the decisions for it
- One enters Jesus' Church by becoming a member of his Body, which comes by being born again through believing/responding to the Good News
- Each believer was made a king under Jesus and a priest under Jesus (of the Melchizedekian order, a priesthood higher than the Levitical priesthood, see Hebrews 7)
- Each believer was given specific function(s) in the Body, necessary to all, so there is to be no schism in the Body. Also, no part's function is more necessary than another part's. Even, "the Head can't say to the feet I don't need you" (1Cor 12:21)
- Each believer was given the Great Commission, as mentioned earlier. This included signs, which follow their preaching, and the responsibility to teach people. The first believers all preached and taught, as we'll look at later on
- Each believer was created in Christ Jesus to do specific

works prepared for them beforehand (Eph 2:10), and each receives knowledge/faith to do these works (Rom 12:2-4)
- Jesus gave apostles, teachers, evangelists, prophets, and shepherds as gifts to his People. According to Ephesians 4:7, this was associated with the liberation of his disciples and to *train* them to do their works of service (the same Greek word translated "ministry," which shows that according to the Bible every believer has a ministry)
- Elders were appointed in Churches/cities in order to "oversee" (or "supervise"), the believers there. They were to shepherd the flock. To be given this office they had to pass a character test.

Regarding this last point, we need to carefully look into Scripture to clear up some traditional misunderstandings. There is an office in the Body of Christ called elder. We see it, for example, in Acts 20:17-38, where Paul addressed "the *elders* of the Church" in Ephesus (vs. 17). He said this to them:

Acts 20:17-18, 28 (NKJ): [Paul] sent to Ephesus and called for the *elders* of the Church...he said to them...take heed to yourselves and to all the flock, among which the Holy Spirit has made you *overseers*, to *shepherd* the church of God which He purchased with His own blood.

Notice the three terms associated with this role: elder, overseer, and shepherding. Let's look at each of the three.

The term, "<u>elder</u>" implies further growth, maturity. However, there was more to it than that. Elders in the Hebrew society at the time of Jesus and the apostles, as in many ancient societies, were advisers and worked together to solve problems in their community. They had recognized authority for the people of their city or town, and they worked together to care for them.

The elders of a city in Israel would sit at the gate of the city (see Prov 31:23, Joshua 20:4). They were qualified in this role by their maturity and demonstrated character (e.g., Prov 24:7). The gate was the place of protection for the city, and from it, elders would watch out for those in their city. It was also where the elders formed a council to discuss pressing matters relating to their people (e.g., Prov 24:7). Disputes could be settled at the city gate (e.g., Duet 22:15), and judgment rendered (e.g., Duet 22:24).

This reveals for us the power of a council or councils of elders, which regularly meet together, pray together, and make decisions by the Spirit together for the well-being of the flock in their city. Apostles present in the city should be part of this as well, just as we see in Acts. Several times it documents a group consisting of "the apostles and elders," meeting to work out difficult problems.

In the Scripture above, the term, "<u>overseer</u>" is used to identify the elders. Paul said to the elders, "God made you overseers." An overseer is a supervisor. It's someone who watches work being done by others and provides leadership support using a broad perspective.

The term, "overseer" is a literal translation of the Greek word, "episkopos," which is sometimes translated "bishop." The difference is that "overseer" is a translation of the meaning of the word, and contains in it a description of the job. On the other hand, "bishop" came into English by the sound, rather than the actual meaning.[3]

Regarding the third term, an "overseer of a flock," is a "shepherd." Paul said to the elders, "the Holy Spirit has made you overseers, to <u>shepherd</u> God's Church in Ephesus." Shepherding includes caring for, protecting, and guiding a flock of sheep. Shepherds in the Middle East generally move their flocks forward as they walk behind them. The main job of Elders was to oversee and shepherd God's People in the city they were located.

"Shepherd" in Greek is the exact same word often translated "pastor" by us today ("pastor" comes from Latin). Because the two terms evoke very different ideas in people's minds, I use "shepherd" when speaking of the Scriptural

---

[3] In other words, through *transliteration*, which allowed the actual meaning to be lost and a traditional meaning raised up in its place.

ministry. This is the original, Biblical meaning. The term "pastor" to most of us has a meaning at least partially by tradition, and it can potentially limit us from all God has for us.

The rest of the New Testament Scripture is in agreement regarding the three aspects of this post among God's New Covenant People. The apostle Peter addresses elders this way:

1 Pet 5:1-2, 4 (NKJ): The *elders* who are among you I exhort, I who am a fellow elder [Gr., "co-elder" or "associate elder"]...*Shepherd* the flock of God which is among you, serving as *overseers*...and when the Chief *Shepherd* appears, you will receive the crown of glory that does not fade away.

In another place, Paul also calls elders overseers:

Titus 1:5-7 (NASB): For this reason I left you in Crete, that you would set in order what remains and appoint *elders* in every city as I directed you, namely if [anyone] is above reproach, the husband of one wife, having children who believe, not accused of dissipation or rebellion. For the *overseer* must be above reproach...

So we see that God wants elders to be appointed as overseers, in order to shepherd the Church and Flock of God.

Having more than one name to identify the same ministry is not unique to elders. Evangelists also are referred to in Scripture as both "evangelists" and as "reporters" (KJV: "heralds") (Lk 9:2, 6; Ac 8:5; 1Tim 2:7).

Furthermore, elders are not the only ones in the King's Body who are specifically called to shepherd. Ephesians 4:11 speaks of a spiritual gift/service that is simply called, "shepherds." We will cover that gift to the Body in Part 4 of this book, and I think you'll be amazed and blessed at our findings. For now though, let's continue to look into the lost role of elders.

Chapter 4
More on Elders of God's Churches

It's noteworthy that though elders were to oversee the others, they were of the same group—brothers and sisters. Elders were commanded not to "lord it over others" but to "be examples to the flock" (1Pe 5:1-4). This shows that they had a visible position of leadership that *could* potentially be used to lord it over others, though they weren't supposed to do so. They were, rather, to identify with the group of sheep and be examples for them—to do the same as the older ones did.

Not all elders are teachers (see 1Tim 5:17). Some may be teachers in addition to their office of elder. Some may be gifted as prophets or have any number of callings. But *all* are called "*overseers*" of the *flock* of God, and *all* are commanded to *shepherd*. It was understood that elders in a city would shepherd the Flock there.

To be able to oversee a believer's growth requires having gone through the gamut of Christianity oneself, having survived and grown through "the good fight of faith." So to become an elder, a person will need to go through this at least once, for the sake of testing. Though he will face ongoing testing of his faith through various testing, having made it through victoriously at least once gives a person the ability to see where a younger believer is on his or her journey.

So elders require a serious evaluation before being appointed (or "ordained") through the Spirit with the laying on of hands. A list of requirements in Scripture isn't given for evangelists, teachers or others, though they also must grow up into their callings over time. They're also warned of greater judgment because of greater responsibility, but I think the list is clearly provided for elders because they are accountable for the souls of God's People, and they can protect, or fail to protect, sheep from the going astray of teachers, prophets, and others.

Here is the character test used to prove potential elders' maturity:

1 Tim 3:1-7 (NASB): It is a trustworthy statement: if any man [lit., "anyone"] aspires to the office of overseer, it is a fine work he desires to do. An overseer, then, must be above reproach, the husband of one wife, temperate, prudent, respectable, hospitable, able to teach, not addicted to wine or pugnacious ["contentious"], but gentle, peaceable, free from the love of money. He must be one who manages his own household well, keeping his children under control with all dignity (but if a man does not know how to manage his own household, how will he take care of the Church of God?), and not a new convert, so that he will not become conceited and fall into the condemnation incurred by the devil. And he must have a good reputation with those outside Church, so that he will not fall into reproach and the snare of the devil.

Titus 1:5-9, 11 (NASB): For this reason I left you in Crete, that you would set in order what remains and appoint elders in every city as I directed you, namely, if [anyone] is above reproach, the husband of one wife, having children who believe, not accused of dissipation or rebellion. For the overseer must be above reproach as God's steward, not self-willed, not quick-tempered, not addicted to wine, not pugnacious [i.e., "contentious"], not fond of [deceitful profit], but hospitable, loving what is good, sensible, just, devout, self-controlled, holding fast the faithful word which is in accordance with the teaching, so that he will be able both to exhort in sound doctrine ["healthy teaching"] and to refute those who contradict...[who] must be silenced...

We see in both of these passages that "anyone" can become an elder. If one aspires to this office, it's a good thing. He should be welcomed by current leadership in this decision, then taken through this character test thoroughly. In the context of appointing elders, Paul wrote:

1 Tim 5:22 (NASB): Do not lay hands upon anyone too hastily and thereby share responsibility for the sins of others; keep yourself free from sin.

From this and other verses, we can understand that the appointing of elders includes both a human and spiritual element. As we saw in Acts 20, the Holy Spirit is involved: "the Holy Spirit has made you overseers." Also the person himself is involved: "If anyone aspires to the office of overseer" (1Tim 3:1). And current leadership is involved as far as taking a person through the character test and "laying hands upon" the person to appoint them (see 1Tim 5:22).

Let's look at another verse about elders, those who "watch out for" (oversee) believers' souls:

Heb 13:17 (NKJ): Obey those who rule over [Gr., "lead"] you, and be submissive, for they watch out for your souls, as those who must give account.

The term translated here as, "rule over," in Greek is "hegeomai," meaning, "to lead." It includes the idea of leading/bringing/driving to a destination. This is what shepherds do with a flock. They make sure they get there.

Similarly, in 1Timothy 5:17 Paul speaks of "the elders that rule well" (NKJ). Here the Greek word for "rule" is "proestemi." The first part, "pro," means "before" or "in front of." The next part, "stemi," means "to stand." So it means "to stand before." In other words, "The elders who stand well, before God's People..." This is *not* the Greek word used of secular ruling. Rather it seems to mean standing in sight of the others so they will also be able to stand. In the context of a journey, it would also include leading the way and taking the persecution and tribulation first.

In 1 Thessalonians 5:12-13, Paul says, "know them who labor among you and are over you in the Lord and admonish you." Here, "are over you" is the same word as mentioned above, "prostemi." It should read, "who labor among you and stand before you in the Lord."

These mistranslations in the King James Version are tragic because they go against Jesus' command of how to serve his People (Lk 22:25-27). There is a submission to these leaders required, but it's primarily out of fear of Christ, not fear of the human (Eph 5:21, 1Pe 3:6).

How then can leaders keep order and get the flock to obey if they can't manage them from above as in the case of a human governmental system or organization? This is a great question. Paul spoke about this in Romans, chapters 1 and 16. He stated that his purpose among the Gentiles was to bring them to, "the obedience of faith." In other words, "Who is Paul? Who is Apollos? Only servants through whom you believed" (1Cor 3:5). They brought the Word, with love, by the Spirit, with power, and those who heard it were then accountable to it. They could choose to obey God by the faith put in their hearts through the Word.

Many times Paul "pleaded" with Churches. This shows he didn't rule over them with human intimidation. It was up to them to choose whether or not to keep walking on the narrow path. He also didn't feel he owned them or had an exclusive right to them. He didn't run off the other servants who came in to build on the true foundation. His attitude was that the Churches were God's possession; he called them, "The Churches of God" (1Cor 11:16, 1Thes 2:14, 2Thes 1:4). He taught that if someone comes to build on the foundation, he'll be judged for his work by the Lord (1Cor 3:10-15). He watched out for, warned, and gave his input to Churches. He even judged false ministers by the power of the Spirit at times (e.g., 1Tim 1:20), but he was careful not to lord it over the Churches he worked with or try to make them obedient by human force (2Cor 1:24, Mt 20:25-28).

Another illustration for us of how spiritual authority

works: Paul served the Word to people, "with a demonstration of the Spirit and power" (1Cor 2:4). Christ accomplished through him, "the obedience of the Gentiles by word and deed, in the power of signs and wonders, in the power of the Spirit" (Rom 15:18-19). Paul taught, "The Kingdom of God is not in word but in power" (1Cor 4:20). That same power could be used to punish evil, but it was power from God; it was not human power. True spiritual authority must work this way.

Each city in Acts eventually had elders. After evangelism, eventually an apostolic team would appoint elders in the cities. Paul told Titus he left him in Crete, "to appoint elders in every city" (Tit 1:5). On another occasion, after evangelizing from city to city, Paul and Barnabas, "appointed for [the disciples] elders in every Church" (Ac 14:23). Notice that the Churches existed before elders were appointed. But the way Jesus instructed apostles to help him build his Church was to appoint elders as overseers to shepherd the flock.[4]

Early on, apostles will play an active role in the oversight of Churches, including elders. Paul instructed Timothy on how to receive an accusation against an elder, also how to discipline them if need be (1Tim 5:19-21). If no apostles are offering oversight to elders, the elders themselves can still implement Biblical instructions such as these. So we see that elders need to support each other and keep each other accountable.

The protective aspect of overseeing and shepherding makes elders gatekeepers to the city for the Church. Traveling ministers must go through the overseers, so to speak. They become friendly contacts to the good ministries, but the counterfeits should feel the pain of the elders' shepherding staff—whether through direct confrontation or prayer. The Spirit will help overseers accomplish this gatekeeper work in order to protect the flock.

The believers in a Church were to know who at least some of the elders in their city were (1Thes 5:12). They were also to have access to more than one of them to call on when facing

---

[4] Notice that the elders in Ac 14:23 were relatively young believers, though they had grown faster than some others in their cities and were stable.

challenges they couldn't handle. If they faced a sickness too powerful for them, they were to call several elders to come and help (Jas 5:14).

In summary, elders are a wonderful provision to God's People whose Scriptural job includes:

1. "Taking care of the Church of God" (1Tim 3:5)
2. Working together as a team with other elders and the co-elders[5], providing accountability to each other and an example of unity to all
3. Overseeing the work of the Gospel, ensuring each member is participating and fulfilling their ministries (Ac 20:28, 1Pe 5:1-4)
4. "Shepherding" God's Flock (Ac 20:28, 1Pe 5:1-4, Heb 13:17)
5. "Leading" (lit. Greek of Heb 13:17)—part of shepherding, includes idea of leading/bringing/driving to a destination
6. "Standing before" God's People (lit. Greek of 1Tim 5:17 and of 1Thes 5:12)—providing stability and a visible example of perseverance and faith (see also Heb 13:7)
7. Holding on to the true Gospel, in order to exhort disciples with healthy teaching and refute and silence false teachers in the community (Tit 1:9-11, 1Tim 3:2)
8. "Diligently laboring among" disciples and "admonishing" them ("gently cautioning and reproving" them) (1Thes 5:12)
9. Being available to give counsel and prayer to God's People (Prov 31:23, James 5:14)
10. As gatekeepers to the city, allowing good ministers in and keeping the wolves out (Prov 31:23, Joshua 20:4, etc.)

Elders are extremely powerful, constant, and stable forces of God in an area. They can be an example of godliness consistently over long periods of time. They can persistently beat on the enemy's kingdom in a city. Their presence, consistent example of standing, their shepherding, oversight, and the ministries they bring in provide an oasis for believers in

---

[5] We will cover the Biblical term, "co-elders" in the next chapter.

their city to find relief, nourishment, and growth in. They can also provide a resting place for traveling ministers who may need to settle down for a while. Thank God for this office! They provide a service for disciples in a city that apostles, on the go, could never do, nor could teachers, evangelists, or prophets.

It seems clear to me that if an elder moves to another city, he may not be qualified to formally oversee the Church of God there right away. He may not be older than most believers there; he may not have overcome the spiritual opposition unique to that city. If there is leadership already present, ideally he should be tested again to be welcomed into the council of elders and publicly recognized as an elder of the Church in this new place. I'd say if he was an elder somewhere else, good leadership of any place he moves to will gladly test him with the goal of recognizing him as an elder there too. The laborers are few.

Chapter 5
Apostles & Elders Work Together

Since the elders were responsible for the Church in their city, they worked together for the common goal of fulfilling the Great Commission there. As they worked for the evangelizing of "every person" in the city, they also oversaw the growth of the disciples there. Eventually, the Spirit was able to set apart people as apostles to go from that city into new territories, unreached by the Gospel (e.g., Ac 13:1-5). They would take the Good News to a place, use great wisdom to lay the foundation of Jesus' Church there, and eventually appoint elders. With prayer and fasting, they "commended them to the Lord they'd believed in" (Ac 14:23). In other words, these elders weren't dependent on the apostles as much as on the Lord, and they were under the Lord's covering or "umbrella."

In Acts, over and over the expression is used, "The apostles and the elders." The two groups worked together. The outward spread of the Gospel caused a need for the appointing of many elders. We see them spring up almost instantly in Acts. Many of them must have been from the 120 who had followed Jesus to Jerusalem and then stayed in the upper room.

Once appointed, the elders *worked with* the apostles. The apostle Peter referred to himself, literally, as a "co-elder," in 1Peter 5:1. The Greek word used is "sumpresbuteros," a "co-presbyter," in other words, a "co-elder" or "associate elder." I understand this to mean that when he returned to where he'd laid the foundation for a Church, he operated alongside the elders there. He didn't lord it over them nor position himself over them, since he'd already, "commended them to the Lord in whom they'd believed" (there's no higher authority than him). So, apostles functioned as co-elders, alongside the elders in cities which already had the Gospel.

Still, the apostles were fathers to the Churches they established, including the elders there. They undoubtedly served the elders while with them, as well as the rest of the Church. They had spiritual authority to do so. But they were only allowed by the Lord to be servants who worked alongside the Church, in helping them continue on. At one point in a letter, Paul had to teach the Corinthians that he was their father through the Gospel—it's possible he had never taught them that before. We see that he wasn't trying to make a name or secure a position for himself. He wanted them to spiritually discern his authority and place in their life.

Apostles in the Word of God are not only called, "co-elders." They're also specifically called overseers. It was said about Judas that when he died he forfeited his "office of overseer" (Ac 1:20, KJV: "bishoprick"). So apostles are also overseers. We can also see that apostles worked in teams, as did elders in a city. Timothy, Titus, Mark, and Silvanus are some of those who worked with Paul and Barnabas. Those who were part of these teams would help oversee Churches alongside elders, as we read of Timothy and Titus doing in Paul's letters to them.

The main difference between apostles and elders is that apostles (Gr., "sent ones") often go, and elders stay. Also, apostles lay the foundation of Churches, including the initial appointing of elders, whereas elders supervise the work after it's already begun. Apostles in Acts also continued to offer service such as oversight and teaching to the new Churches, including the elders, from time to time, at least for a while. It would depend on the need and opportunity as to how long an apostle would continue to offer oversight and service to a Church.

Apostles function primarily in the spread outward of the Gospel and elders in the maturing of believers where the Gospel has already spread. Again we need both—the spread outward as well as the maturing of those who've believed.

Elders don't necessarily go to totally unreached areas with the Gospel, but they have the task of helping the believers in their city get the message to everyone there.

Though elders are mainly appointed to make sure believers in a city mature, they contribute to the spread of the Gospel outside their cities as well, as the maturing believers learn to offer prayer and funding to apostles who go. Elders can also ensure that the believers they oversee become the material that the Spirit can call apostles out of. Apostles pray for the Churches they've founded and may go back to them over time to see how they're doing and offer help. So the two offices work together for both the maturing of disciples and the expansion of the Kingdom into unreached areas.

Among the apostles and elders in Jerusalem in the book of Acts, the person who stood out most in regard to authority was Jesus, through the Holy Spirit. Room was made for the Holy Spirit to transmit the mind of Christ, the Head. Everyone else was on a level plane and looked up for his wisdom ultimately. They could not afford to look to a certain person more than others—what if the Spirit wanted to speak through someone else this time?! They wanted to get things right because they really wanted to please their risen King and also because if they didn't, it could mean death at the hands of persecutors.

If you think about it, if it wasn't for Jesus initiating this new way of leadership, none of us would have the slightest chance. If he didn't voluntarily go down to the lowest level to boost us up as kings, we would have no right to him. He's way too high. He requires all of us to take the same attitude and approach (Phil. 2:5-11), especially leaders, those who are to be examples of doing so.

The Bible never distinguishes between the maturity levels of elders through titles. Of course elders varied in maturity levels and giftedness, but such was discerned spiritually among them, through humility, relying on the Holy Spirit. So they never called Peter the "Senior Apostle," nor were there levels of elders given different titles. If someone was operating powerfully, they would recognize that and make room for it. They didn't need to create an office to solidify that. They wanted to stay on the same level, as leaders, all looking up to Jesus and ready to be led by the Spirit.

This was a very powerful practice. Proverbs commends "the shephanim," a little creature it calls, "exceedingly wise" because "it makes its home in the rocks" (Prov 30:26). With the power flowing through Peter as things got started, he needed to not be distinguished as higher than the other apostles and the elders. After stepping up, like in a council meeting, and speaking the Word of the Lord powerfully or doing something else that was glorious, he needed to be able to sit back down among the others, to sink back into rank with the other apostles and elders, as a brother to all the believers. It was a cloak of humility, for his own soul and his image with others. This helped him to "not think of himself more highly than he ought, but rather with sober judgment" and to "not be proud, but be willing to associate with people of low position; [to] not be conceited" (Rom 12:3, 16). As Jesus said, "You have One Teacher and *you are all brothers*" (Mt 23:8). Looking up at Jesus we're all on the same level.

The first leaders in the Church wanted to be exalted by God through receiving his grace. He gives it to the humble, and "everyone who humbles himself will be exalted" (Mt 23:12). They knew Jesus' teaching that if they made themselves first in this age, they'd likely be last in the next. They wanted a reward in the next age, rather than only having the one here of being admired of men.

Chapter 6
Holy vs. Unholy Ambition

There are various unholy ambitions that exist in the souls of fallen men. One of them is in regard to preeminence and greatness. Jesus dealt with this wrong way of thinking in the twelve, the first apostles, and it was publicized for all of the early Church to see. It was also written for our benefit:

Mark 9:33-35 (NIV): They came to Capernaum. When he was in the house, he asked them, "What were you arguing about on the road?" But they kept quiet because on the way they had argued about who was the greatest. Sitting down, Jesus called the Twelve and said, "Anyone who wants to be first must be the very last, and the servant of all."

So the kind of ambition Jesus revealed for his People to have is very different than the world's way. We see more here.

Matt 18:1-4 (NASB): At that time the disciples came to Jesus and said, "Who then is greatest in the kingdom of heaven?" And He called a child to Himself and set him before them, and said, "Truly I say to you, unless you are converted and become like children, you will not enter the kingdom of heaven. Whoever then humbles himself as this child, he is the greatest in the kingdom of heaven."

This holy ambition is that of humbling ourselves, and Jesus

exemplified it for us:

Phil 2:3-9 (NASB): Do nothing from selfishness or empty conceit, but with humility of mind regard one another as more important than yourselves; do not merely look out for your own personal interests, but also for the interests of others. Have this attitude in yourselves which was also in Christ Jesus, who, although He existed in the form of God, did not regard equality with God a thing to be grasped, but emptied Himself, taking the form of a bond-servant, and being made in the likeness of men. Being found in appearance as a man, He humbled Himself by becoming obedient to the point of death, even death on a cross. For this reason also, God highly exalted Him, and bestowed on Him the name which is above every name...

Jesus went down to the lowest, so God raised him to the highest. The way up is down. So rather than looking up and trying to find ways to get ourselves higher, we just need to use our abilities to serve others more. It will actually kill the selfish ambition in us and store up for us treasures of eternal glory.

Satan exemplified for us the danger of selfish ambition. He looked up and tried to get a higher position for himself, to satisfy his craving for it. He sought a way to lift himself up higher than where God had put him. When he then tried to grasp equality with God, God threw him far down.

The answer is to look down and serve more, instead of seeking a higher status or identity (in truth we already have the highest identity: in Christ). We see Jesus' example again on this issue:

John 13:3-5, 12-17 (NIV): Jesus knew that the Father had [given all things into his hands], and that he had come from God and was returning to God; so he got up from the meal, took off his outer clothing, and wrapped a towel around his waist. After that, he poured water into a basin and began to wash his disciples' feet, drying them with the towel that was wrapped around him... When he had

finished washing their feet, he put on his clothes and returned to his place. "Do you understand what I have done for you?" he asked them. "You call me 'Teacher' and 'Lord,' and rightly so, for that is what I am. Now that I, your Lord and Teacher, have washed your feet, you also should wash one another's feet. I have set you an example that you should do as I have done for you. I tell you the truth, no servant is greater than his master, nor is a messenger greater than the one who sent him. Now that you know these things, you will be blessed if you do them."

Part 2: In Desperate Need of Reform

Chapter 7
Indications of Our Present "Wretchedness"

I am an optimist. When I think of the Church on Earth at this time, I often think of how it is the best off it's been in hundreds of years. Comparing it to the Dark Ages, we have so much more of what God intends for his People. Thank God for such light and life!

I heard one servant of God who is well traveled say he believes there are more men and women of God on the planet now than have ever been in history. Though there is also a lot of negative, we can still be super-optimistic!

- Famous actors, actresses, musicians, and sports figures have publicly been born again in many countries, undoubtedly the result of praying Christians and the spread of the Gospel
- Great revivals have broken out in many places of the world
- In one city I know of, an entire gang was converted to Jesus[6]
- Some makers of pornography have been converted and now help others get free from that trap[7]
- Modern praise music has developed and facilitates more

---

[6] *Transformations: A Documentary* (The Sentinel Group, 1999), DVD.
[7] Shelley Lubben, *Truth Behind The Fantasy Of Porn* (USA: Shelley Lubben Communications, 2010).

praise to God corporately and privately
- Great resources have been produced which are helping marriages and families succeed, despite great difficulty
- Good teaching can be found by believers now through conferences, books and other ways not available in the past
- People are much freer to leave and/or think past their denominations than in generations past
- Healing & miracles, like those recorded in Acts, have been restored to the God's People in many places and are increasing
- There are precious gems of truth now available in many parts of the Body of Christ on Earth. Like gold refined in the fire, these have become more and more pure over time

I used the word, "wretchedness" in the title of this section because of what Jesus said to the Church in Laodicea. Despite the good we can see and must remember, in many cases Churches in politically free countries seem to closely resemble this Church rebuked in Revelation. Jesus said to it, obviously in great love, pity and hope:

Rev 3:17 (NKJ): ...You do not know that you are wretched, miserable, poor, blind, and naked.

Paul said the attitude of mature believers should be that of not thinking they've arrived at perfection. They are to press on (Phil 3:12-16). Most or all denominations started out as movements that were restoring a lost truth to the Body of Christ. Often they were persecuted by other believers for it, by those who had become proud and content with their own previous achievements. At the point at which organizations or movements solidify and stop pressing on, they forfeit the ability to grow further and usually become an enemy of those who would do so. Many or most of them failed the "success test," the hardest test of all, just as the Church in Laodicea did.

The changes I am writing in this study are to be implemented with humility and a desire to continue to grow. Once we see the Spirit respond to some of these changes, we will experience some success. Refreshing always follows repentance (Ac 3:19). That's when there will be temptation to boast in comparison with others, to stop, and to solidify. To do so is to lose. Solidifying usually goes along with creating a name to identify the movement and beginning to overly celebrate and promote it. Doing so isolates the restored truths or benefits into just one part, but the Lord seeks to bring them back to his whole Body on Earth.

After solidifying, the next step is to accuse others who are less knowledgeable or advanced. At this sad point, additional light will often be rejected. We all have to guard ourselves against this. We're called to serve each other. If you get a new truth, write it on others' hearts, and help them walk correctly so they will eventually teach others. In time it can go out into the whole Body of Christ this way.

There are many indicators that we are in great need of change:

- The Great Commission, Jesus' last instruction to us, is not commonly being carried out as Jesus commanded. It includes the evangelism of every person, various signs following the believers, new converts being trained as disciples, and these disciples eventually participating in this outreach
- It's been reported that more believers from the United States are leaving the mission field than joining it
- Our public evangelism has very low retention rates (some estimate around 85% failure rate). In other words, many being "joined to the Church" by God through the new birth do not find the traditional groups of believers in their city appealing enough to meet with
- When Jesus operated in Israel, the prostitutes and criminals were attracted to him. It was mainly the religious hypocrites that hated him. In our cities and towns, often prostitutes and criminals are deathly afraid to come to us for help. And we don't typically go to them. We seem to be more like the religious hypocrites in this way than like Jesus
- Most Christian meetings are made up of a high percentage

of women and low percentage of men.[8] Since women are not intrinsically more holy than men, this is an indication of a problem with our system and/or message
- It's not uncommon for believers' children to go astray. It's very common actually. So evangelism and discipleship are not even happening in many believers' own homes, much less outside
- Often sincere and precious believers end up marrying unbelievers, to their great regret. This reveals a lack of teaching, oversight, encouragement, fellowship, and prophecy, etc. for single believers
- Several times Paul wrote of different topics, "I do not want you to be ignorant of this." Of most of these topics, almost all Catholic, Orthodox, and Protestant believers (including Evangelical, Pentecostal, Charismatic, etc.) are ignorant today. This shows that vital teaching and Bible reading is clearly lacking among us
- Very few believers in a church group know or walk in their specific callings or functions in the Body of Christ (some estimate 1% or less). This shows a lack of true worship and renewing of the mind, according to Romans 12:1-2. It also shows people aren't being equipped to do the works prepared by God for them, *and* that place isn't being made in the meeting or church structures for their ministries. The People of God and the lost world are suffering unnecessarily because of this
- Few believers rise to places of political power or media influence in their societies. There is very little visible effect of Christianity, in terms of honesty and morality, on the designing or marketing of products or services. Unbelievers running companies are not afraid to lose potential customers based on Christian values. For example, out of all the large hotel chains, none stand out nationally for offering rooms without pornography. There is no believer who has risen to that level of influence. In general, believers take

---

[8] David Murrow, *Why Men Hate Going To Church* (Nashville, TN: Thomas Nelson, Inc., 2005), 4.

more servant roles in businesses. I believe this is because of a pawn/peon mentality, resulting from our traditions in church structure, which I will cover extensively in this book
- In many countries, unbelievers don't fear the presence of God in his Church, though they did in Acts at one time, nor do they physically persecute believers, as they later did in Acts. Since the Church rejoiced for being counted *worthy* of such persecution (Mt 5:11-12, Ac 5:41), many of us are evidently lacking and as of yet, "unworthy" of it
- The United States and several other countries at this time could be called nations of backsliders. Doing outreach, you encounter many people who have been born again in the past but went astray. They found joy and fulfillment in Jesus, and they regret not walking with him now. They are confused about what was missing and why they didn't keep on with Christ, and they just figure they were wrong. However, I have stayed with Christ myself, and though I definitely say they should have stayed, there are also problems with our current system that contributed to their falling away. We must identify and address these. The backsliders are not necessarily the only ones at fault

Chapter 8
Recent Revelation from God Regarding Reform

When the Spirit was poured out on the Day of Pentecost, God began speaking more frequently to his People through prophecy, visions, and dreams (Ac 2:17-18). Because the benefits of this are unlimited, there is a counterfeiter who would love to deceive us or at least murky up the waters. All revelation other than Scripture must be tested. Also, though I believe the revelations I've recorded here are true and edifying, I obviously do not endorse everything these people I've quoted may teach or do. We're taught by Paul, "Do not quench the Spirit; do not despise prophetic utterances. But examine everything carefully; hold fast to that which is good" (1Thes 5:19-21).

About 12 years ago, a friend of mine who's a prophet relayed to me what was told him by revelation from the Lord, that Martin Luther reformed some of the doctrine of the Roman Catholic Church but not much of the structure. The structure of the Church still needs to be reformed.

While preaching and teaching in India recently, I was hosted by an older man of God who I consider a teacher and a prophet. I lived with him nearly two months and testify to his faith and love. He told me of a revelation he had from the Lord, that he is coming soon and his Church needs to be reformed in order to reach the nations and so his Bride can be prepared to meet him when he returns.

Another teacher and prophet came to a nearby city, and I heard him speak. He related a vision he had seen of a typical church. He saw it as a day care center. There was more to the vision, but the parallel I could see between a day care center and our typical church-organizations is that the children are without the care of parents. Also, most are being managed by outward pressure of rules and laws, just as un-regenerated people are by their organizations and governments. They are not being trained through the Spirit to live for God from the inside out, nor given responsibility and raised up. They're being babysat and spoon-fed—in some cases just for money. Furthermore, in daycare parents are separated from their children. Our current structure typically doesn't foster a direct personal relationship with God the Father. It's also rare that believers in it receive the care of fathers or mothers of faith.

The Lord shared with a famous author something he was going to do (according to Amos 3:7). He said, "I am about to restore the ministry of pastor (shepherd)." This brother was shocked as he'd assumed that was the one ministry we actually *do* understand. As we'll see through this book, the Biblical shepherding ministry has been buried under the rubble of the Dark Ages for a long time.

I heard about an African American prophetess who was sent into a meeting of pastors to tell them the Word of the Lord: he wanted to move, and they needed to get out of the way and let him do so. I took that to mean that they were in the way by being positioned over the people. The people were looking up to each of them as the one who ministers and, therefore, they sat still and did nothing. But it seems to me God wanted these men to "step down" in a sense, and thereby to elevate God's People to the place of freedom and the recognition of their dignity and personal responsibility to do their appointed good works. Then God could move through them all.

In another instance, a church-group fasted for forty days, including Thanksgiving and Christmas. At the end of that time, a pulpit was supernaturally lifted up into the air and ripped in two without human influence.⁹ The tear would've been impossible for humans to make, as it went across the grain of the unique fiberglass design. I have not heard more on that incident, but I have always wondered if those believers reformed their meeting after that or if they went back to business as usual. It seems to me that the Lord was communicating to them, and us, a need for change. I believe Jesus wants his place among us back.

I was part of a church-organization for a couple years in which a man had the traditional role of the pastor and was controlling. In this setting, a friend of mine had a vision or dream in which she saw everyone in the group dressed in plain brown clothing. However the leader moved on stage, they all moved in unison. There was another man, also a leader among the group, who was dressed in different clothing in the vision and was therefore squeezed out of leadership. This was an accurate picture of what was going on, including a certain leader being rejected. The traditional pastor was gifted as a teacher and so, according to tradition, people gave him the role as Head. By doing so and focusing on him, they were more conformed to his image than to the Lord's, I'd say. People lost their individuality. I can also say we lost our ability to fulfill our own ministries. Eventually, God got me out of there, and out of love I've prayed for this man and group to be blessed and get free. My journey into and out of that group turned into a very valuable lesson for me, and I mention this because it is *very* common in our current structure.

I spoke to another prophet recently who related me what the Lord had once told him, to never cause people to seek to obey him over the Lord himself in their lives and to *never* build up a following in order to sustain financial support.

Recently, I was handed a prophecy given in and partly about Portland, Oregon: "I am raising up a leadership such as the earth has not seen before…I'm going to raise up prayer and healing schools—not just from one church, but it's going to be

---

⁹ Tommy Tenney, *The God Chasers* (Shippensburg, PA: Destiny Image Publishers, Inc., 2001), 8.

spread across this city, and people will come in and they'll say, 'No, I'm not just going to go here, I'm going to go there,' and the Lord says, 'I'm going to do it so many places in this city that the devil can't stamp it out.'"

I have a good friend with whom I've done outreach for a couple years and can testify of his sincerity and gifting. He related to me a vision he had:

> I was sitting at my desk, resting my head on the desk, when suddenly I was transported to a street (at this point, I didn't know if I was in or out of my body). I stood opposite a house, and I heard the Spirit say to me, "Consider this house." It was a big, beautiful, two-story house. But I also noticed it had a busted window and shudders in disrepair.
>
> Then I was transported into the house, and I found it to be in total disrepair. The entire inside was gutted. There was building debris everywhere, and all the walls were laid down. (see Mt 23:27). As I considered what could be done about it, the Spirit told me, "Look down." I then realized I was standing on a big, solid rock, which was the house's foundation. I knew it would never be moved and never be shaken (see Mt 16:18). Then the Rock rose up and filled the house!

Another close friend of mine had a dream on 14 July 09, while I was writing this book. This brother's been a believer for about 40 years and has served in both traditional and non-traditional forms of ministry. When he told me about the dream, he had no idea it corresponded so well with the message of this book. It follows:

> I was with a dozen or so people, out in a forest. We were looking at a small building that had been abandoned and had weeds and brush growing up all around it. Inside it had cobwebs and spiders and dust everywhere. It was built with small inadequate boards, like a playhouse or something, and some of the boards were rotting. We were

inspecting it to see if we could fix it up and use it to meet in. The more we looked, the more hopeless it appeared. I was reaching up and pulling pieces of rotten board off and suggested we just burn some of it off. We tried to burn off the rotten part, but it was just too dangerous and nearly set the whole structure ablaze before we put the fire out. I then woke myself up saying, "maybe we aren't ready for the fire yet!"

I got up and prayed for a time. I knew it was the Lord and the message was pretty clear: our existing structures were not adequate for a fresh move of the Spirit. I lay back down and went to sleep, and again I was in the same dream. This time we had moved a little ways away, cleared land, and built a new structure. It was strong and large and had room to build on and expand every side. It was not ornate, but clean and usable. I was amazed at how fast this structure went up; it seemed like hardly any time at all, and it was there. I was walking through it saying, "This is it! This is going to work. We finally got it right." And the dream ended.

Later, this friend had a dream related to coming changes in how believers meet, and I've recorded it for you in Chapter 28.

Chapter 9
Why Do Traditions of Men Go Down So Hard?

When Jesus came to Earth he was pure light, but he faced opposition from men and evil spirits. Much of what he had to fight through were the traditions of men. He pointed to them as the problem several times. Tradition was one of the reasons the leaders in Judea sought to kill Jesus (Jn 5:16). Why is it so powerful?

2 Cor 10:4-5 (NKJ): ...the weapons of our warfare are not carnal but mighty in God for pulling down strongholds, casting down arguments and every high thing that exalts itself against the knowledge of God, bringing every thought into captivity to the obedience of Christ.

Traditions can become fortified strongholds for the enemy to hide out in and fight from. They can shape and form our thinking so that we reject the truth when God sends it to us. The result is what Jesus encountered and exposed:

Mark 7:8-9, 13 (NKJ): For laying aside the commandment of God, you hold the tradition of men...All too well you reject the commandment of God, that you may keep your tradition...[you make] the word of God of no effect through your tradition which you have handed down...

Traditions can become assumptions we make regarding the will of God. They can become false light for us in that way, which we rely on (Prov 21:4, Jn 9:40-41). They can become things we do to seek to establish our own righteousness, and they can be used to accuse others. We have to be very careful with them. Again, they are among the *main* things that motivated many in Israel to kill Jesus. They are not sins usually, but they often become the cause of sins. Relying on them, instead of the counsel of the Lord, is wrong (Prov 3:5-6).

Satan, knowing all this, utilizes traditions as a tool. He tries to raise them up and cause believers to lean on them in order to keep us from fulfilling God's purpose. They can be so subtle that they are like secret traps set up for us to fall into and be limited by. Traditions are often counterfeits of what God really wants.

A traditional concept or practice is one that is not rooted in the truth of the Gospel, but relied upon as if it is.

To illustrate how difficult it is to tear down traditions, an English author once relayed a piece of English military history. When the British fought the United States in the US Revolutionary War, the British army fought as they always had: they would march out in rank to the beat of a drum, wearing highly colored uniforms. They could not conceive of any other way of fighting. Their past successes actually helped reinforce their blindness, so that any suggestion otherwise would have been rejected at that time. The result was thousands of casualties, as the Americans hid in the swamps and shot those soldiers down from the trees.[10]

In order to hold to our traditions, many of us often still crucify Jesus today. It happens when God plants in a person something that doesn't fit the mold. As that little believer tries to bring it to fulfillment, those strong through human religion and tradition try to kill it. Too often they succeed. We need to humbly, meekly, blindly follow the Holy Spirit in such a way that the traditions in us that are offensive to God will be torn down.

---

[10] Derek Prince, *Spiritual Warfare*, in *On Experiencing God's Power* (New Kensington, PA: Whitaker House, 1998), 469.

From my viewpoint, our Christianity today is riddled with the most tradition in the areas of 1) leadership structure, 2) meeting format, and 3) financial giving. We need to be very careful and honestly link our teachings and practice with plain teaching of the Scriptures. If our teaching on a subject is compulsory, it *must* be plainly taught in the Scripture. Secondly, even if it's a clear message in the Scripture—specifically in the New Covenant, written to believers—it must be taught in a non-condemning, non-condescending way. All of us are susceptible to a serious consequence if we're not careful. We *all* need to fear the Lord in this:

Prov 30:5-6 (NKJ): Every word of God is pure...Do not add to His words, lest He rebuke you, and you be found a liar.

Chapter 10

What Does God Really Require?

We need to simplify back to where we know what God really wants. How are we considered right by him? What does *He* require? We need to not let our traditions ever cross with the truth of the Good News.

How are we made righteous through Christ? God's righteousness is given to us through Jesus' sacrifice and God's raising him from the dead—and it's accepted by faith. "The righteous will live by faith." We believed the message we heard, so God reckoned us righteous and we were made alive. We're all alive now, in Christ. We're members of his Body, united by being such. We're part of the New Man, the New Creation. It happened simply—through believing and submitting to the message we heard, the Good News about Jesus the Christ, the ruler God sent to save and reconcile the world. Our sins were forgiven and we were given his righteousness. ☺. There's no death sentence for us anymore. We've been given LIFE by God's grace.

The enemy will come with a tradition or doctrine or requirement of written law to make us righteous. He's trying to bring us death (2Cor 3:6, Rom 7:8-11). He may try to use the Law of Moses. The Gospel teaches that even the Jews who believed were released from it, through Jesus' death and resurrection (see Rom 7:1-6), and are now under the new law (1Cor 9:20-21). Or he may use a traditional law formed by Gentile Christians who've forgotten they were made righteous by faith.

The New Covenant has a new law (see Heb 7:12, 8:8-13, Jer 31:31-34). It's "The Law of the Spirit" (Rom 8:2). It's also referred to as, "The Law of Liberty," in which the Spirit engrafts the Word into our hearts (Jas 1:21-25, 2Cor 3:3-18). It's carried out by being led by the Spirit, walking by the Spirit (Rom 8:14, Gal 5:25). We now have an obligation to the Spirit (Rom 8:12-13).

If we stay in the Spirit, yielded to the Spirit, the Guide who Jesus sent to lead us, we will have and develop the "fruit of the Spirit," which is "love, joy, peace, patience, kindness, goodness, faithfulness, gentleness, and self-control. Against such things there is no law" (Gal 5:22-23). This is what God wants in us, not just the observance of outward laws. In the New Covenant, God writes his laws on our hearts by the Spirit (Heb 10:16-17, 8:8-12). He leads us into all truth.

John 1:17 (NKJ): For the law was given through Moses, but grace and truth came through Jesus Christ.

Rom 7:4, 6 (NASB): Therefore, my [Jewish] brethren [who know the Law (acc. to vs. 1), you] were made to die to the Law through the body of Christ, so that you might be joined to another, to Him who was raised from the dead, in order that we might bear fruit for God...we have been released from the Law, having died to that by which we were bound, so that we serve in newness of the Spirit and not in oldness of the letter.

So the requirement first of all, for helpless humanity (Rom 5:6-8), is to sincerely believe the Good News. That's all God requires to grant his "gift of righteousness" (Rom 5:17) to them:

Rom 4:5-8 (NKJ): But to him who does not work but believes on Him who justifies the ungodly, his faith is accounted for righteousness, just as David also describes the blessedness of the man to whom God imputes righteousness apart from works: "Blessed are those whose

lawless deeds are forgiven, and whose sins are covered; Blessed is the man to whom the Lord shall not impute sin."

Eph 2:8-9 (NKJ): For by grace you have been saved through faith, and that not of yourselves; it is the gift of God, not of works, lest anyone should boast.

The way people are to respond to the Good News initially is by confessing Jesus as their Lord and then being baptized (Rom 10:9-10, Mk 16:16, Ac 10:48). From that point, new believers are called to the life of discipleship. Paul says they have become "slaves to righteousness" (Rom 6:18). In other words, they have an obligation to the Spirit:

Rom 8:12-13 (NIV): Therefore, brothers, we have an obligation…[to the Spirit].

We must *walk* by faith to be right before God in our lifestyle (though we've already received his righteousness). We must obey his commands:

1 Cor 7:19-20 (NKJ): Circumcision is nothing and uncircumcision is nothing, but keeping the commandments of God is what matters.

Gal 5:6 (NKJ): For in Christ Jesus neither circumcision nor uncircumcision avails anything, but faith working through love.

1 John 3:23-24 (NKJ): And this is His commandment: that we should believe on the name of His Son Jesus Christ and love one another, as He gave us commandment. Now he who keeps His commandments abides in Him, and He in him. And by this we know that He abides in us, by the Spirit whom He has given us.

1 John 5:3-5 (NKJ): For this is the love of God, that we

keep His commandments. And His commandments are not burdensome. For whatever is born of God overcomes the world. And this is the victory that has overcome the world—our faith.

Eph 2:10 (NKJ): For we are His workmanship, created in Christ Jesus for good works, which God prepared beforehand that we should walk in them.

John elsewhere calls this, "walking in the light" and thereby having fellowship with the Father, Son, and fellow believers. This walk is not in darkness—no darkness is allowed. He also said the test of this lifestyle is whether we love God, our brothers/sisters, and do not love the world (1Jn 2:3-11, 15-17).

By living this way, we eventually fulfill the word God speaks concerning us when we're born again: "his/her faith is reckoned to him/her as righteousness" as we do righteous works by faith (Rom 4:22-25, Jas 2:14-26).

Having said all that let's look again at the cross. When Jesus died on it he released all who would believe from the obligations of the Law of Moses or any other outward law. By doing so he "stripped principalities" of their armor (Col 2:15). Their offensive armor is accusation, but because Jesus became the perfect sacrifice for us and gave us his perfect righteousness—*they lost!* The cross is, therefore, the foundation of our victory. By walking in the Spirit, in view of Jesus' sacrifice, we receive its benefits over time. There's a battle involved, with the principalities and the rest of Satan's kingdom. A main strategy of Satan is to take our eyes off of the cross, where he was legally defeated and where everything good was given to us:

Gal 3:1-2 (NKJ): Foolish Galatians! Who has bewitched you that you should not obey the truth, before whose eyes Jesus Christ was clearly portrayed among you as crucified?

2 Cor 11:3 (NKJ): ...I fear, lest somehow, as the serpent deceived Eve by his craftiness, so your minds may be

corrupted from the [sincerity] that is in Christ.

Satan's scheme is to subtly influence certain individuals who will then "bewitch" (curse) those who are free to walk by the Spirit. How do they do this? Galatians reveals that they do it by taking believers' eyes *off* the cross. How? By introducing something else to focus on and praise most highly.

Gal 6:14-15 (NKJ): But God forbid that I should boast except in *the cross of our Lord Jesus Christ*, by whom the world has been crucified to me, and I to the world. For in Christ Jesus neither circumcision nor uncircumcision avails anything, but *a new creation*.

Col 2:8 (NKJ): Beware lest anyone cheat you through philosophy and empty deceit, according to the tradition of men, according to the basic principles of the world, and not according to *Christ* ["*the Messiah," "the King"*].

The result of Jesus' becoming our sacrifice on the cross and our receiving it by faith, is that we were given full forgiveness and freedom from sin (Ac 13:39, Rom 6:6-7). Acknowledging this, we are able to walk according to our new life given by grace, with the faithful help of the Holy Spirit, so that "There is therefore now no condemnation for those who are in Christ Jesus" (Rom 8:1). It's a great privilege.

We see the victory of Jesus' cross in this next verse:

Col 2:11-15 (NKJ): In Him you were also circumcised with the circumcision made without hands, by putting off the body of the sins of the flesh, by the circumcision of Christ, buried with Him in baptism, in which you also were raised with Him through faith in the working of God, who raised Him from the dead. And you, being dead in your trespasses and the uncircumcision of your flesh, He has made alive together with Him, having forgiven you all trespasses, having wiped out the handwriting of requirements that was against us, which was contrary to

us. And He has taken it out of the way, having nailed it to the cross. Having disarmed principalities and powers, He made a public spectacle of them, triumphing over them in it.

When Paul here states the powerful effect of the cross for us against all the spiritual enemies of God, he then gives us a resulting responsibility of extreme importance. In the next verse he writes:

Col 2:16, 18 (NKJ): *So let no one judge you* in food or in drink, or regarding a festival or a new moon or sabbaths, which are a shadow of things to come, but the substance is of Christ. Let no one cheat you of your reward…

The enemy will try to raise up distractions from the cross to carry believers off. He wants us to rely on the Law of Moses or our traditions for security with God, when God's approval comes from his gift of righteousness by faith and, subsequently, walking by the Holy Spirit in love, according to truth.

If a believer is walking this way and enters a church-organization, he may possibly cross people's traditional ideas and ways of doing things. He may not fit the box. If they embrace him out of love and adjust to make room for him, they've walked according to righteousness and by the Spirit. But if they accuse and reject him based on their traditions, they've shown themselves to have already lost their footing on the foundation of the forgiveness of the cross and our obligation now to love one another.

A temptation we may encounter is to be so concerned with keeping our religious concepts and rules that they end up condemning and separating us from *fellow believers* who Christ died for, because we think differently on disputable matters. In this way, we can actually condemn ourselves because we've then departed from love. We have to boast only in the cross and choose to love and serve all of God's People. We all got in through the same grace—we're to "accept one another as Christ accepted us" (Rom 15:7).

If our eyes move off the cross onto something else as our boast, we will become overly conscious and zealous for that thing. We will think we've got something great because of our knowledge or practice of it, but in actuality, our lives will be more desert-like spiritually than in the past when we simply had Jesus. We will become easily offended by other Christians who disagree with us on that point, and separate from them (which is to reject them).

I've seen Christians *divide* from others based on traditions concerning what human organization they are or are not a part of, whether or not they meet in a traditional building on a traditional day of the week, whether or not they like the same particular Bible teacher, whether they eat foods that were unclean under the Law of Moses, disagreements about how much Christians should give financially as a minimum, how or if they celebrate certain feasts. It's very subtle how the cross can be obscured by minor issues, not necessarily related to love and obedience to God. Jesus died and rose so we could be righteous apart from law (Rom 3:21-22), united in love (Jn 13:34), and growing in the fruit of the Spirit (Gal 5:22-26). It wasn't so we'd reject each other over side issues. "Love…is not provoked [and] endures all things" (1Cor 13:5, 7).

Rom 14:17-18 (NKJ): For the kingdom of God is not [about] eating and drinking [or other outward laws not related to the fruit of the Spirit], but righteousness and peace and joy *in the Holy Spirit*. For he who serves Christ in these things is acceptable to God and approved by [spiritual] men.

To recap, then, God requires the cross. Subsequently, he requires that we walk by the Spirit. Acknowledging the cross and the New Creation is prerequisite to being led by the Spirit (Rom 6:11, 8:1; Gal 5:24-25). So we need to keep these in view, staying away from things designed to make us "fall from grace" (see Gal 5:3-4) to an earthly, human-law level. Trying to be righteous by external rules and traditions is actually denying the power of Jesus' cross and the sufficiency of the Spirit of Truth.

Heb 13:9 (NKJ): Do not be carried about with various and strange doctrines. For it is good that the heart be established *by grace*, not with foods which have not profited those who have been occupied with them.

If we can do this, we will live on a supernatural plane, by the Spirit, and the result is "that the requirement of the Law may be fulfilled in us" (Rom 8:3-4). Notice that the word, "requirement" here is singular. This is the *one* requirement which the Old Covenant Law and the Prophets hung on (Mt 22:40). It could not be fulfilled in people without the cross and the Spirit because of the problem of flesh (Rom 8:3). This is the same requirement that sums up the New Covenant Law, written on our new hearts by God's Spirit. It's *love*.

1John 4:7-12 (NKJ): Beloved, let us love one another, for love is of God; and everyone who loves is born of God and knows God. He who does not love does not know God, for God is love. In this the love of God was manifested toward us, that God has sent His only begotten Son into the world, that we might live through Him. In this is love, not that we loved God, but that He loved us and sent His Son to be the propitiation ["the satisfying sacrifice"] for our sins. Beloved, if God so loved us, we also ought to love one another.

Chapter 11
How Our Structure & Meeting Practice Changed

After the New Testament was written, significant changes were made to what the Lord set up in regard to leadership approach and meeting style. Traces of these changes can be found as early as the second century A.D., and they gradually became the status quo over the next couple hundred years. These eventually resulted in "the Dark Ages," a time in which the simple truths of the Gospel and the fulfillment of the Great Commission became very scarce in Europe and elsewhere.

According to Ephesians 6:12, we must see all of what happened as a Satanic plot to stop the progressing dominion of God's Church, which was spreading throughout the world, steamrolling Satan's kingdom with the authority of Jesus the Anointed King.

The Enemy's scheme worked—temporarily and from one perspective. Thankfully, Jesus and others had prophesied these challenges for us beforehand (Mt 13:24-36, Ac 20:29-31, 1Jn 2:18-19), and the end is glorious, absolutely GLORIOUS! ☺. The Church will be perfected and prepared, without blame or blemish or wrinkle—suitable to marry the Lord Jesus Christ when he returns (Eph 5:25-32, Rev 19:7-8).

Let's take a look at some of the changes that were made in the first few centuries after Jesus left. I've broken the list into two categories—leadership approach and meeting style.

Regarding *leadership approach*:

- A hierarchy was introduced into Christianity, with various levels of man-appointed authority. Titles were created or misused to identify the new levels: "bishop," "presbyters," "deacons," "arch-bishop," "priest," "nun," "monk," etc. In Scripture, the office of elder is synonymous with overseer (Old English: "bishop"), and they were to shepherd (Old English, "to pastor"), as we covered in Chapter 3.
- A separation was imposed on groups of believers through two new identities put on them: "clergy" and "laity" (or "parishioners"). The Biblical identities given to each believer of being a king (whether male or female), under Jesus the King of Kings, and a priest, under Jesus the High Priest, were lost. So disciples didn't exercise their spiritual authority anymore nor directly enter the presence of God anymore
- Jesus, the only mediator between God and man, the only Head of the Church in Scripture, was no longer the focal point relied upon in this system. Believers stopped looking up to Jesus as their direct mediator and started looking to the clergy. Consequently, they lost the guidance and power of the Holy Spirit (remember, a "different spirit" goes with a "different Jesus" and a "different gospel")
- Eventually, a man was raised up and identified as "the bishop" (later called "the priest") of each group. People, therefore, began to look to him as higher than them. So the truth unique to the New Covenant: "no longer will a man teach his brother saying, 'know the Lord' for they all will know me, from the least to the greatest" (Heb 8:11) was lost, in addition to many other truths
- The Scriptures were eventually banned from the public, those not "ordained," and Christianity became more of a form than a life-giving relationship with God through Jesus

Regarding *meeting style*:

- As Christianity became more institutional, evangelism stopped. Rote ritual became the norm, without the Great

Commission as a vision and goal
- Meetings of believers began to be conducted only in public places, no longer in homes at all. A separation was, thereby, created between "church life" and personal, home life
- The elaborateness of meeting places became a focus and ambition. The most elaborate meeting building would be visited and favored by the emperor when he visited a city
- Eventually, "holy" buildings would become "churches." However, in Greek the word "church," when used for Christians, refers to a *People* who are called out from the world to rule for God. The true Christian sanctuary today is in the literal temple of God, in Heaven (Jn 4:23-24; Ac 7:48; Heb 9:24, 10:19-22), and us as His People (1Cor 3:9,16-17)
- As a result of the new building and public meeting focus, oversight of believers' actual lives ceased. What people did away from the building became unknown and their individual spiritual growth unaccounted for
- Meetings took on a theater-style form and began to follow a certain set program. The Spirit was no longer relied on in the ordering of the meetings
- The Gospel ceased being taught to people as the messages were eventually given only in Latin (this is one of the problems John Wycliffe, Martin Luther and others helped reform—thank God)
- Only the "priest" would speak in meetings, so the New Testament exhortations to, "teach one another, encourage one another," couldn't be practiced. The New Testament model of having meetings in which, "everyone has a hymn, a teaching, a revelation, a spiritual language or an interpretation," a prophecy, a psalm, a spiritual song, etc., as described in 1Corinthians 14:26, Ephesians 5:19, and elsewhere in the New Testament, ceased

These structural changes that crept into God's Church made it a wineskin unfit to hold the Spirit and introduced a multitude of evils among us. Although the Reformation in Europe in the sixteenth century brought back much of the Gospel to the world (thank God), it did not reform the leadership approach or meeting style. This is a job we must do. As we reform our structure and practice, we will subsequently remove many mental shackles we've experienced for centuries.

Part 3: Rediscovering the Basics

Chapter 12
Jesus Has a Vision

All believers and groups of believers are called to unify under Jesus himself. He is THE Truth. He's superior to the various truths our human organizations are often united around. Once united under our common Head, by way of each calling him Lord and accepting one another as he accepted us, we will eventually all share his vision and work together toward it. I use the term, "vision" here loosely to mean overall purpose, mission, or goal.

The Tower of Babel in the Bible is one of the things "written for our instruction" in this age (Rom 15:4). It was written as a warning for us because if we're not careful we can practice the same rebellion as the builders of that tower. They became proud and chose to ambitiously build upward to make a name for themselves, rather than be fruitful, multiply, spread outward and fill the earth as God had commanded. They were rejecting the commission of God for their age. The Commission God has given us is more complete and includes subduing Satan's kingdom and setting human captives free in all nations of all the earth.

Since Jesus is the Head, he has the privilege of providing our vision. He did so when he gave us the Great Commission just before he left. It includes two parts. Half of it is *evangelism*:

Mark 16:15-17 (NKJ): Go into all the world and preach the gospel to every creature. He who believes and is baptized

will be saved; but he who does not believe will be condemned. And these signs will follow those who believe...

John 20:21-23 (NKJ): So Jesus said to them again, "Peace to you! As the Father has sent Me, I also send you." And when He had said this, He breathed on them, and said to them, "Receive the Holy Spirit. If you forgive the sins of any, they are forgiven them; if you retain the sins of any, they are retained."

Luke 24:46-49 (NASB): And He said to them, "Thus it is written, that the Christ would suffer and rise again from the dead the third day, and that repentance for forgiveness of sins would be proclaimed in His name to all the nations, beginning from Jerusalem. You are witnesses of these things. And behold, I am sending forth the promise of My Father upon you; but you are to stay in the city until you are clothed with power from on high."

Ac 1:8 (NASB): ...but you will receive power when the Holy Spirit has come upon you; and you shall be My witnesses both in Jerusalem, and in all Judea and Samaria, and even to the remotest part of the earth.

The other half of the Great Commission is *training the new disciples* who've believed:

Matt 28:17-20 (NKJ): When they saw Him, they worshiped Him; but some doubted. And Jesus came and spoke to them, saying, "All authority has been given to Me in heaven and on earth. Go therefore and make disciples of all the nations, baptizing them in the name of the Father and of the Son and of the Holy Spirit, teaching them to observe all things that I have commanded you; and lo, I am with you always, even to the end of the age." Amen.

When Jesus said, "teaching them to observe *all things* I have commanded you," he included this Commission. So there is to be a growth process in every believer, just as in the original twelve. It ends in teaching others who will also carry the Gospel out to unbelievers and teach others, who will also evangelize and teach others...to the ends of the earth.

Before the end of this age, this Commission will be completed, as prophesied by Jesus the Anointed King:

Matt 24:13-14 (NKJ): But he who endures to the end shall be saved. And this gospel of the kingdom will be preached in all the world as a witness to all the nations, and then the end will come.

In the end, those who have labored toward the Great Commission's completion will receive a great reward. Those who haven't will miss the reward. The endurance required in completing this Commission, given to all believers, is what will prepare each one to be included in the Bride of Christ and Marriage Supper of the Lamb. Those who align with Jesus' vision and endure in doing so are "making themselves ready" for that (Rev 19:7-8). What an opportunity we have!

If Jesus were the CEO of a company, who went on a long business trip, came back, and examined our work, he'd find we are, for the most part, not accomplishing the mission he gave us. Our money and time do not generally go toward spreading the Gospel to the unreached in our cities and towns but toward buildings in which we who already believe can meet. Generally speaking, our goal has been to have meetings in these buildings in which a few people minister and the vast majority continually receives ministry. But the Great Commission included a responsibility for every believer to minister.

We need to each align ourselves with Jesus' vision, and then he will lead us on how to accomplish it. Building traditional-church buildings may not be the best way because Jesus already said, "Go" to his disciples. We're instructed primarily to "go", rather than build something in order to attract people to come to us. My city has 1.5 million people. If the goal is to take the powerful Good News to them all, constructing buildings to attract people would be the last method used. First, they're very expensive. Second, they can only fit a very small percentage of the amount of people we're supposed to reach in our city. Third, many people will never be willing to enter them because of the negative stigma attached to them. But Jesus, the Head, will reveal to us ways to evangelize everyone if we align with his vision to do so.

Likewise in discipleship, Jesus' way of making disciples was not by building a big building and teaching an hour or two a week. It was and still is hands on. Large buildings may be very useful, but we need to be careful to work according to Jesus' Commission and not get sidetracked, as is very easy to do.

There is a counterfeit to the Vision of the Lord that crept in through Roman Catholicism and other traditions. It is to get a nice looking building, fill it with people, sit them down, and teach them for the rest of their lives. If a person comes and listens for 30 or 40 years, he's considered a faithful brother. This is whether or not he has taken up his cross and fulfilled his calling from God. In the Roman Empire, this became the norm as evangelism was stopped and a religious ceremony took the place of Christianity. The goal was to be faithful to "the church," not to the Lord. In other words, people were expected to attend meetings, pay money, and generally not be troublemakers. Since the leaders set this expectation, the people fulfill it. But it's not even close to what the Lord requires of his disciples.

Today, many well-meaning believers are confused. They attend a meeting on Sunday because they think it's what's required of them as Christians. They may give 10% of their money as well, if they believe that is required of them. They go home and try to live a decent life, often struggling with things they can't seem to overcome, and they are confused as to their calling. So they just try to be good people and "go to church." But an unshakable awareness of condemnation and unfulfillment exists in them. They know they were born again and experienced Jesus at that time, but they're bored. A major reason is that the gifts of God given them for the fulfillment of the Great Commission are dormant within them.

The attendees know that there is a taste of Life in the meetings. This is usually because of the praise time and/or the gifting of the speaker, but *it's not enough*. The reason they feel this way is because they are not walking in the Lord's calling for them to contribute to the fulfillment of his Commission. They are not being taught, trained, nor allowed, through facilitation, to contribute.

The traditional church-organization leaders may feel they are doing right because everyone else does the same and seems to have always done the same. Also, they notice the same Life the attendees do on Sunday morning. They figure the whole thing has God's approval, and they continue on. They can fall into a trap of contentment, based on the salary they receive from those who attend meetings. (They need our prayers, not criticism). This contentment is so dangerous, as it's what caused the leaders of Israel to reject and kill Jesus. They had no desperation and felt no need for change and for God's Messiah, so they missed him.

The subject of healing and miracles is an interesting one. Evangelists often see great results among unbelievers as Jesus backs up the Gospel they preach with signs following (Mk 16:20). Servants of God who try to get believers in traditional church-groups healed often face greater difficulty in doing so. God wants to heal them, but they need to align with his will. There they will find the measure of faith given to *them* to fulfill his calling for them (Rom 12:2-4). And as they "seek first the Kingdom of God and his righteousness" all they need will be added to them.

There are individual callings for each believer which are their personal visions in helping complete the Lord's Vision. One common problem in traditional church-organizations is that often a man is put in the place of the Head. Therefore, the whole group is expected to share that man's vision instead of the true Head's Vision. This may lead to great frustration for the man as he tries to get the others on board with his vision (rather than the Lord's Vision and their individual callings). Or, if he's strong enough, it may cause everyone to give up their individual callings to try to help him fulfill his goals.

That we can know our Head's vision is such a great provision from God. It's a stress reliever for our souls when things get confusing on our journey. We can just stop, align ourselves with Jesus' vision, and know we're on the right track. There are a variety of distractions that can try to take the place of Jesus' vision. They may sound good, but we need to stay on track with what he *actually* said: *evangelize* and *make disciples*.

Paul aligned his purpose with the Lord's Commission. The following is how he worked to fulfill the discipleship aspect of it.

Col 1:28-29 (NKJ): [Christ] we preach, warning every man and teaching every man in all wisdom, that we may present every man perfect ["mature"] in Christ Jesus. To this end ["for this *purpose*"] I also labor, striving according to His working which works in me mightily.

Often our goal is to get people to regularly attend our meeting, or at least some church meeting. But Paul's goal was that Christ would be formed *in* people (Galatians 4:19). The emphasis should be on the people themselves, what they do at home and how they carry out their entire lives. This is a shift in focus we need to make. It means a lot more work, but if Christ is formed in people, it means they will join to help in the work as they move according to Christ in them. Of course we should also bring them into a community of believers, but that will include much more than most believers are typically being offered today.

Paul wanted to present people "perfect." The Greek word also means "complete" or "mature." Among other things, maturity in Christ Jesus is indicated by the following.

- Restraining & taming the tongue (Jas 3:2)
- Endurance in trials, without grumbling (Jas 1:4)
- Being continually led by the Spirit (Rom 8:14: "sons," not "children," implies maturity)
- Being peacemakers (Mt 5:9) who stay unified with other

believers (Jn 17:23, Eph 4:13, Col 3:14: "love is the unifying bond of maturity")
- Having developed spiritual sensitivity to do right and having become able to handle "meat," that is, the parts of the Gospel related to responsibility, self-denial, endurance, and accountability at the Day of Judgment (Heb 5:14)
- Consciously working to fulfill their part in completing the Great Commission (Mt 28:20)

Once mature, disciples are to keep pressing on to reach further maturity and the ultimate goal of Christianity, which they also must recognize that they haven't reached yet (Phil 3:8-15).

These next two passages show Paul's deep and ongoing commitment also to the evangelistic part of Jesus' Vision:

1 Cor 9:16, 22 (NKJ): ...woe is me if I do not preach the gospel...I have become all things to all men that I might by all means save some.

Acts 20:23-24 (NKJ): ...the Holy Spirit testifies in every city, saying that chains and [afflictions] await me. But none of these things move me; nor do I count my life dear to myself, so that I may finish my race with joy, and the ministry which I received from the Lord Jesus, to testify to the gospel of the grace of God.

Chapter 13
What Does "Church" *Really* Mean?

Much confusion has existed over the centuries as to what the Christian Church is and our obligations to it. Many have been martyred over this subject. In history, many have condemned themselves and others over this very misunderstood subject, and many still do today. To get clear we need to go back to the source—the Scriptures—to determine what a "church" actually is. I invite you to look back with me.

The word, "church" is actually a mistranslation. It does not convey the meaning of the Greek word, "ekklesia." In examining the makeup of this word, we find the first part, "ek," means "out of," and the second, "klesia," means to call. So it's related to being called out of a larger group, into something not everyone can participate in. For this reason, some have said ekklesia means simply, "a called out group." For several years this was the only understanding into the word I had. But actually it's not the full meaning of the Greek word. It's only the makeup of the word.

The word ekklesia in the Greek language and culture of Jesus' day meant, *specifically*, a *ruling, governing assembly*, a *legislative body*, which exercised *authority* in the city.[11] Most Greek cities had

---

[11] Derek Prince, *Rediscovering God's Church* (New Kinsington, PA: Whitaker House, 2006), 25; E.J. Forrester, *The International Standard Bible Encyclopedia, Vol 1* (Grand Rapids, MI: WM. B. Eerdmans Publishing Co., 1956), 651; R.C. Trench, *Synonyms of the New Testament*, 7th ed., 1-2; Oskar Seyffert, *A Dictionary of Classical Antiquities*, 202-203; www.britannica.com /EBchecked/topic/177746/Ecclesia;http://dictionary.reference.com/brow

them. They existed in both the Greek and, later, Roman empires. Only certain people in these cities were qualified to be in them. These people were "called out" of the rest of society and into the governmental assembly. For example, requirements to be in the Assembly of Athens included being an adult male, a citizen and born free. An "ekklesia" was the central authority of the city government, with power to veto or approve every decision for the city.

So "ekklesia" is a political term, *not a religious one*. If translated according to its meaning, the English term used would not have been "Church" but something like "Royal, Governing Assembly," or "Legislature." In this regard, it is not parallel to the synagogue of Israel. There are a few similarities, but the New Covenant, Governing Assembly is much more authoritative and powerful.

We can see a Biblical example of the political aspect of ekklesia in Acts 19. This is one of the few places the King James and other versions translate "ekklesia" according to its actual meaning. The setting is Ephesus. The spread of the Gospel and the power of God eventually caused believers to bring out and burn the equivalent of $9300 US Dollars worth of occult books (Ac 19:19). Idolatry was being destroyed, and it affected those who made money manufacturing and selling idols. That's when Demetrius tried to put a stop to it all:

Acts 19:24-25 (NKJ): A certain man named Demetrius, a silversmith, who made silver shrines of Diana, brought no small profit to the craftsmen. He *called* them together with the workers of similar occupation...

Notice how he "called" out a group? And look next at where they went—to the theater, where political and other formal gatherings were held.

Acts 19:29 (NKJ) ...the whole city was filled with confusion, and rushed into the *theater* with one accord...

---

se/ecclesia?s=ts.

Acts 19:31-32 (NKJ): Then some of the *officials* of Asia, who were [Paul's] friends, sent to him pleading that he would not venture into the theater. Some therefore cried one thing and some another, for the *assembly* [Gr., *ekklesia*] was confused...

In the end, it took the *city clerk* (vs. 35) to shut this unlawful *ekklesia* down:

Acts 19:38-39 (NKJ): "...if Demetrius and his fellow craftsmen have a *case* against anyone, the *courts* are open and there are *proconsuls*. Let them bring charges against one another. But if you have any other inquiry to make, it shall be *determined* in the *lawful assembly* [Gr., *ekklesia*]."

Do you see how the political aspect of "ekklesia" is brought out in the context of these verses? Now what if the word "church" was used in these verses, as in other times ekklesia is translated into English in the New Testament? It wouldn't make sense to us because we see "church" as a religious term meaning an organization or gathering of Christians, when really there's *a lot* more to it.

So where did this word, "church" come from? The word ekklesia was not translated into Latin; it was *transliterated*. This means a new word was created according to the sound of the Greek word. This is sometimes done for the sake of convenience. It can also be done to cloak the meaning of original words. An example of a transliteration for convenience is the Chinese dish, "Chow Mein." It was transliterated from Chinese to English according to its sound, rather than its actual meaning in Chinese, which is "stir-fried noodles." As for "ekklesia," it was transliterated into Latin as "ecclesia," according to the sound, rather than translated into a Latin word meaning "governing assembly." Once the original meaning was lost, a totally new one could be constructed in its place. This is what happened. What was the motive?

We need to understand that the original Roman Catholic

Church-organization was joined very closely to the government of the Roman Empire, from the fourth century onward. The Roman Empire considered itself the greatest kingdom and one that would never end. Thus, it sought to stamp out any notion of another kingdom superior to it, namely the Kingdom of God. To say that Jesus has a Kingdom, not of this world, which is administered by supernatural power through his Governing Assembly operating in many nations of the Earth—that was unacceptable to Rome. Therefore, truth about the Kingdom of God was cloaked, including the meaning of "Christ" as "Anointed King" ("Messiah"), the fact that he will come back and rule here, and the identity of his People as his Royal, Governing Assembly on Earth.

By the time the Bible was translated into English, tradition had already shaped believers' thinking in this area. Also, there were no longer citywide governing assemblies operating as there had been in previous empires. So rather than translate ekklesia into English as "governing assembly," or "legislature," the King James Version and others used an English word, "church" (Old English "kirk," "circe," or "cherche"). This word was not a translation or even a transliteration of ekklesia. It had been transliterated previously from a totally different Greek word, "kuriakon,"[12] which means simply, "Lord's" ("Lord" in Greek is "kurion"). Kuriakon is used in the New Testament twice, in "The *Lord's* supper" (2Cor 11:20) and "The *Lord's* day" (Rev 1:10). So though it was not an accurate translation, nor even a transliteration of the Greek word "ekklesia," this is how the modern English word "church" came about.

Some languages that came out of Latin retained Latin's transliteration of ekklesia (e.g., in Spanish it's "iglesia"), though the meaning had been long forgotten. Possibly no translation, in any language, has captured the original meaning of ekklesia. But somehow, out of all the rubble, praise Jesus that we are regaining this truth today!

The Kingdom of God directly confronts the kingdom of Satan (Mt 12:28). The enemy does not want us to know this

---

[12] www.merriam-webster.com/dictionary/church.

truth about our identity as God's Governing Assembly because if we know who we are, we will, naturally, correspondingly act it out. We will exercise our heavenly authority against him!

This political aspect of who we are as a group is in line with many New Testament Scriptures that describe our new identity in the King ("Christ"). Here are a few of them:

1 Pet 2:9 (NKJ): But you are a chosen generation, a *royal* priesthood, a holy nation, His own special people, that you may proclaim the praises of Him who *called you out* of darkness into His marvelous light.

Rev 1:5-6 (NKJ): ...Jesus Christ...the ruler over the kings of the earth...who loved us and washed us from our sins in His own blood, and has made us *kings* and priests to His God and Father, to Him be *glory and dominion* forever and ever. Amen.

Rom 5:17 (NKJ): ...those who receive abundance of grace and of the gift of righteousness will *reign* in life through...Jesus [the Anointed King].

Our whole mindset will change if we hold on to this truth about the ekklesia, God's Ruling People. Notice how the following Scriptures make more sense and give a different feel when ekklesia is translated as "Legislature," according to its true meaning:

1 Cor 1:2 (NKJ): To the *Legislature* of God which is at Corinth...

1 Cor 6:1, 4 (NKJ): Dare any of you, having a matter against another, go to law before the unrighteous, and not before the saints? If then you have judgments concerning things pertaining to this life, do you not appoint those who are least esteemed among the *Legislature* to judge?

1 Cor 12:28 (NKJ): And God has appointed these among

the *Legislature*: first apostles, second prophets, third teachers, after that miracles, then gifts of healings, helps, administrations, varieties of [supernatural languages].

Eph 3:10 (NKJ): ...to the intent that now the manifold wisdom of God might be made known by the *Legislature* to the principalities and powers in the heavenly places.

Eph 5:23-24 (NKJ): ...Christ [the Anointed King] is head of the *Legislature*...the *Legislature* is subject to [the Anointed King]...

Acts 8:1 (NKJ): ...a great persecution arose against the *Legislature* which was at Jerusalem...

Acts 12:5 (NKJ): Peter was therefore kept in prison, but constant prayer was offered to God for him by the *Legislature*.

Acts 15:22 (NKJ): Then it pleased the apostles and elders, with the whole *Legislature*, to send chosen men of their own company to Antioch...

The Legislatures of God were depicted in the New Testament as citywide, as were the earthly, Governing Assemblies of the Greek and Roman Empires. They were extremely powerful forces that ruled spiritually in each city they were located.

Chapter 14
Returning to the Simplicity & Power of Jesus' Legislature

The word, "ekklesia" is used in the Gospels in only two places, first in Matthew 16:18, next in Matthew 18:17. Jesus didn't talk much about it, but what he said was *foundational.*

Matt 16:18 (NKJ): And I also say to you that you are Peter, and on this rock I will build My church [Gr., "My Royal, Governmental, Legislature, My Legislature"], and the gates of Hades shall not prevail against it.

Here King Jesus prophesied to his disciples that he would have a political, governmental assembly of his own, an "ekklesia." He spoke of it in the future tense. He said he would build it, and that it would be engaged in spiritual battle. Also, he said it would be founded on a rock and invincible.

The Greek word for rock used here means a huge, rocky crag/cliff. It's a steep, rugged mass of rock projected upward or outward. The rock, or crag, is Jesus the Christ. Literally, "Jesus" means, "God Saves," and "Christ" or "Messiah" means, "the King/Priest appointed and empowered by God to deliver and rule forever" ("the Anointed One") Also, he is the Son of the living God.

1 Cor 3:11 (NKJ): For no other foundation can anyone lay than that which is laid, which is Jesus Christ.

Matt 16:16-18 (NKJ): Simon Peter answered and said, "You are the [chosen King], the Son of the living God." Jesus answered and said to him, "Blessed are you...for flesh and blood has not revealed this to you, but My Father who is in heaven...and on this rock I will build My [Legislature], and the gates of Hades shall not prevail against it."

Peter received this revelation of Jesus and verbally acknowledged it. This can be done regarding smaller issues and various truths, but in this case Peter did so with THE truth, which would become our great foundation. Whatever is built on Jesus Christ is Jesus' Legislature. Anything off of that Rock-foundation is not qualified. Whatever is on that Rock is invincible spiritually. It overcomes.

The second time Jesus uses the term, "ekklesia," he speaks of it in a localized form. He was teaching what to do if a brother sins against another and won't repent:

Matt 18:17 (NKJ): And if he refuses to hear [two or three witnesses], tell it to the [Legislature]. But if he refuses even to hear the [Legislature], let him be to you like a heathen and a tax collector.

Here he can't be instructing us to tell his whole Legislature, as he referred to in Matthew 16; it's spread out over Earth and Heaven! He means in a certain locality. So within Jesus' whole Legislature, there are smaller Legislatures, separated by physical location.

Jesus then goes on to speak of the *power* granted his Legislature:

Matt 18:18-20 (NASB): Truly I say to you, whatever you bind on earth shall have [already] been bound in heaven; and whatever you loose on earth shall have [already] been loosed in heaven. Again I say to you, that if two of you agree [Gr., "harmonize"] on earth about anything that they may ask, it shall be done for them by My Father who is in heaven. For where two or three have gathered

together in [Gr., "into"] My name ["authority"], I am there in their midst.

We see here that the power works through exercising the King's authority and through prayer because when two or three are gathered into Jesus' authority, he is among them. So what's the smallest possible "Legislature"? It would be two people (for example, if they are the first two believers in a city). Though this may not be common, I believe we need to know that it's all Jesus requires to grant his presence and the power and authority of his Legislature. If two people are both built on the foundation of who Jesus is, through faith, and meet together in order to be in Jesus' Name, they have access to the full power and authority of the King's Legislature. *There are no other requirements* for legitimacy given by Jesus or the first apostles.

We can recognize now that Jesus' Legislature is to be exercising his kingly authority on Earth. In the Old Covenant, the Kingdom of God was given to Israel and it was administered from the physical location of Mt. Zion in Jerusalem. However, the Kingdom was later taken from the nation of Israel when it rejected the King, Jesus. The Kingdom was then given to Jesus' Legislature, made up of all disciples who answer the call into it, from Israel and all Gentile nations (Mt. 21:43). We have together now arrived at the spiritual Mt. Zion:

Heb 12:22-23 (NKJ): But you have come to Mount Zion and to the city of the living God, the heavenly Jerusalem, to an innumerable company of angels, to the general assembly [Gr., "gathering"] and church [Gr., ekklesia, "Legislature"] of the firstborn who are registered in heaven...

We are now, spiritually, on the spiritual Mt. Zion and in the heavenly Jerusalem. And we are the Legislature on Earth of the Firstborn from the dead, Jesus. He is the exalted King of Kings, and at this time his authority is exercised through us on the earth:

Ps 110:1-2 (NKJ): 1 The LORD said to my Lord, "Sit at My right hand, till I make Your enemies Your footstool." 2 The LORD shall send the rod of Your strength out of Zion [specifically, in this age, spiritual Zion, where the Legislature has come to]. Rule in the midst of Your enemies! 3 Your People shall be [freewill offerings] in the Day of your power [or, "army"]. [In holy array], from the womb of the morning, [your youth will come forth unto you as the dew].

In verse 1 here, we see Jesus sitting at the right hand of the Father after his resurrection. His enemies are all under his feet, though they are not made his footstool yet. Then we see in verse 2 *how* Jesus' authority is exercised on the earth now, while the Enemy is still in operation on Earth. Verse 3 goes on to speak wonderfully of Jesus' return to Earth, at the end of this age. But focusing on verse 2, we see that the resurrected, ascended King Jesus rules on Earth now, in the midst of enemies which are still allowed to operate to some extent. He sends out the scepter of his power *through us* on the earth.

The Legislature is King Jesus' Body. It's his extension into the world, the instrument he works through on Earth.

Eph 1:22-23 (NKJ): And He put all things under His feet, and gave Him to be head over all things to the [Legislature], which is His body...

Eph 2:5-6 (NKJ): Even when we were dead in trespasses, [God] made us alive together with Christ (by grace you have been saved), and raised us up together, and made us sit together in the heavenly places in Christ Jesus...

Col 1:24 (NASB): ...[The Anointed King's] body...is the [Legislature]...

As Jesus' Body, we are connected to Heaven through him, and he is connected to Earth through us. He gave us his status as Kings and Priests under him, seated with him on *his* throne.

And he left us on Earth, where we can now, "reign as kings in life through Jesus Christ" (Rom 5:17). He also gave each of us jobs as his various Body parts. So for the Head to accomplish all that he wants on Earth, to use the "all authority in Heaven and Earth" given to him (Mt 28:18), his Body must fully cooperate with him and each other, and each person in his Body must do his or her individual, distinct part.

To fulfill this great calling, we need the Holy Spirit's leading and powerful help. He transmits the directives of the Head to every individual body part. And this is available to us as Christ's Body:

1 Cor 12:7 (NKJ): A [presentation] of the Spirit is given to each [person] for the profit of all [better translation: "to bring all together"].

The Spirit gives each of us a part, a presentation that we use to serve each other when together, and to use to rule spiritually:

1 Cor 12:8-11 (NKJ): for to one is given the [message] of wisdom through the Spirit, to another the [message] of knowledge through the same Spirit, to another faith by the same Spirit, to another gifts of healings by the same Spirit, to another the working of miracles, to another prophecy, to another discerning of spirits, to another different kinds of tongues, to another the interpretation of tongues. But one and the same Spirit works all these things, distributing to each one individually as He wills.

This provision from God, promised to each of us, includes all the supernatural revelation we'll need to make the authoritative utterances on Earth that headquarters in Heaven has decreed (Mt. 18:18). These result powerfully in changes on Earth. Also, the Spirit, along with the Word of God, helps us pray according to God's will so that we receive what we ask (1Jn 5:14-15).

Jesus spoke of the following four operations of his

Legislature:

1. It would engage, victoriously, in spiritual warfare (Mt. 16:18)
2. It would help keep forgiveness, peace, and integrity among its members (Mt. 18:15-17, 21-22)
3. It would exercise Christ's authority while on Earth, by the Spirit of God, through making decrees determined already in Heaven which affect the spiritual and physical realms on Earth (Mt. 18:18)
4. It would engage in unified prayer and receive from God whatever it asks (Mt. 18:19)

These operations are, therefore, all essential and basic to Jesus' Legislature. The main function of the Legislature is to rule.

Now let's compare our concept of "church," passed down to us by tradition, with the characteristics of Jesus' Legislature found in the Scriptures we've looked at. Almost all Catholic, Protestant, and other Christian organizations order their meetings according to a certain form which includes a few key components, done in a certain order. Typically, it looks like this, sometimes with slight variation:

1. Some form of singing/praising
2. Greeting each other
3. Giving financially
4. Hearing a teaching

I propose to you, without contention, that this form is not found anywhere in the Bible (although each of these components *is* found in the Bible and is very valuable). In fact, this form that we have today comes from a sheer tradition of man, which started as an institutional edict in the Roman Empire. Over time, it became synonymous with what we think of as church. We usually call this form either Mass or Service.[13]

---

[13] In the 6th century, "Gregory the Great," a traditional bishop & pope in Rome, created an order of ceremony which became compulsory in all

Please compare these four operations with the four that Jesus ordained, listed above. I'd say the main difference is the purpose of each. (We're dealing with root issues here). The purpose of the first is for the People to be united and extend Jesus' rod into the darkness of the world. The purpose of the second is to praise the Lord and receive instruction. Praise and teaching are essential, as we will see in Part 5 of this book, but this present form alone, misses the point and purpose Jesus laid out for his *Legislature* in Matthew 16 and 18. It's not only to meet in order to sing and hear teaching. It's to allow Jesus to exercise his authority on Earth.

Teaching is a fundamental and necessary ministry for the People of God. However, we need to understand that it is a support ministry for the Legislature's main work. It's not the goal. To illustrate this, consider a large corporation. Part of what goes on internally is the training of employees. It's an ongoing process. Employees will stop their work from time to time to attend training seminars but, then, go back to their work. What if all the employees did was receive training? The company would go under—no matter how good the training.

Our main meetings need to include unified prayer and the exercise of King Jesus' authority by every single believer in attendance, in addition to other activities revealed in Scripture (e.g., singing, prophesying, teaching each other, etc.). If our meetings are not facilitating these fundamentals Jesus spoke about, we are not fulfilling our calling as the Legislature of God.

Reforming from "Church" to "Legislature" will allow us to transition out of a negative image we've fallen into, one of powerlessness. Many unbelievers won't receive Jesus because of this image of traditional-churches, and many good men and women who do believe have a real problem with it as well. The idea is that you take on the role of a passive observer in all meetings. But the risen King's Legislature, with everyone being known as kings and priests unto God and exercising his supreme authority to subdue Satan and rule on Earth each time

---

meetings; Protestant reformers only slightly altered it later.

they meet; with character of love, unity, perseverance, honor, contentment, etc.—this will get the world's attention, and that of everyone else.

We must always remember that as Jesus' Legislature, we exercise the *spiritual* authority of his Kingdom. We do not replace the authority given to physical, human governments by God (see Rom 13:1-7, Tit 3:1, 2Pe 2:13-14). Rather, our authority works on a higher plane than theirs, and we are to heavily influence them through spiritual power (see 2Tim 2:1-2; Lk 12:11-12; Ac 12:21-24, 13:6-12, 24:24-25, 26:28):

John 18:36 (NKJ): Jesus answered, "My kingdom is not of this world. If My kingdom were of this world, My servants would fight, so that I should not be delivered to the [Judeans]; but now My kingdom is not from here."

Once we recapture our identity, as well as the purpose and main activities we're to engage in, once we reform so that each of us is a part of exercising King Jesus' authority on earth, our cities will change. Human government will fear the "lowest" of us (and at times persecute us). Occult practitioners will recognize the true power and spiritual authority of Jesus Christ working in us and surrender to it. We will often be able to expel and prevent evil in educational, political, and media realms. For example, a human leader about to establish an evil law will change his mind after being visited by an angel in his bedroom. We will rule—but it's with spiritual weapons, through unified prayer and the exercise of Jesus' supreme authority by the power of the Spirit.

Chapter 15
Accountability Within The Legislature

As stated in the last chapter, the main function of the Legislature is to rule. Mistreatment of others or un-forgiveness would interfere with contact from the Head, preventing the correct exercise of his authority on Earth. It would also cause disunity in the body, so that it could not "harmonize" and thereby receive answers to prayer.

Jesus *clearly* laid down a procedure to deal with offenses among the Legislature in Mt. 18, which we should reform to. It must be taught to all disciples and practiced, as we see the early believers doing in the New Testament. He said:

Matt 18:15-17 (NKJ): Moreover if your brother sins against you, go and tell him his fault between you and him alone. If he hears you, you have gained your brother. But if he will not hear, take with you one or two more, that "by the mouth of two or three witnesses every word may be established." And if he refuses to hear them, tell it to the [Legislature]. But if he refuses even to hear the [Legislature], let him be to you like a heathen and a tax collector.

On this point, I spoke to good friend recently who told me of his experience, coming from a lawless background. He did well as a believer, and God entrusted him with some amazing power, but sin in the form of drug addiction sidetracked him for a little while. At one point he had to go through treatment provided by the State. He told me he only learned one thing from them, but that was what he needed: accountability. A LOT of our doctrine is really good and effective, but our structure has lacked accountability among members. Jesus purposefully laid this down as a basic part of his Legislature, so we need to practice it.

We see the New Testament Legislatures including this aspect of accountability in 1Corinthians 5, 1Timothy 5:19-21 and 1Thessalonians 3:14-15. Take a moment to look at these passages. This is a necessary provision of God, given to help his People stay on track because although the Old Man is dead, we still face the temptation to not put his deeds to death in our lives.

There should be the knowledge in the back of every believer's mind that if he or she hurts others and doesn't change, someone will address him or her about it. If after that confrontation the person refuses to receive correction, he or she should expect confrontation by the first person and another disciple or two as witnesses. After that, there should be the expectation that the Legislature itself will deal with this next, publicly, if the practice continues. There is to be a fear involved, as in Acts (Ac 5:11, 9:31).

The Legislature is to judge those who are inside it, according to 1Corinthians 5:12-13. In meetings of the Legislature, there must be an open forum for reports like this. This will be a good help for the souls of believers, whose spirits always want to do right. The doctrine of sin being unacceptable and of obedience being required of us will be continually re-enforced in each of our souls if we restore this practice.

Many current sins and gossip about them will be eliminated from among us if we change our thinking and re-implement this practice ordained by the Lord. It may be rare that the Legislature ever has to judge, just as in the New Testament we only have a handful of occurrences of this, because Jesus set this system up mainly as a *deterrent;* it's to eliminate the problem before it gets before the whole Legislature in the town or city.

If we do have to judge, we must keep in mind that the purpose is to keep the sin from spreading like yeast throughout the whole group and to help the person who is sinning (1Cor 5:6-8). The goal is always to restore the sinner—even in the case of a person persisting in rebellion so far that he or she has to be handed over to Satan (see 2Cor 2:5-11). When Jesus implemented this system, the context he set it in was that of restoration and forgiveness—he was speaking of the shepherd that goes after the sheep that went astray and also of forgiving your brother multitudes of times (Mt. 18:10-14, 21-35; see also Gal 6:1).

Jesus was so serious about good relationships among us that he taught us to do something no system in the world would ever do. It will be hard for us to practice this too, but we must obey the King rather than our own desires:

Matt 5:22-24 (NKJ): Therefore if you bring your gift to the altar, and there remember that your brother *has something against you,* **leave your gift there before the altar, and go your way. First be reconciled to your brother, and then come and offer your gift.**

Chapter 16
The Distribution & Boundaries of God's Legislatures

The following is a beautiful picture of a Legislature. Although we see Paul persecuting it in this passage, we can also learn something here about Jesus' Legislature in Jerusalem:

Acts 8:1, 3 (NKJ): ...a great persecution arose against the church [Gr., "Legislature"] which was at Jerusalem...Saul...made havoc of the [Legislature], entering every house, and dragging off men and women...

The one Legislature in Jerusalem depicted here was distributed among many houses. It was *comprised* of all of the believers in Jerusalem and *distributed* in many smaller groups. They all were advancing together, though Jesus was the only one who could see and keep track of all of them.

This perspective is very different than our traditional one. We usually think of there being many Churches in cities that have been evangelized. But God sees *one* Legislature in each evangelized city. As we saw in the last chapter, two or three people gathered into Jesus' Name have access to the King's authority. At the same time, New Testament language suggests that the boundary of each Legislature is the city it's in, just like those of the human governing assemblies. So we see that the People meet in many smaller groups, but all identify with that *one* Legislature. Realizing and recognizing this reality, we will also realize that we are not divided. Competition between smaller groups doesn't make sense, since we're all in the same ekklesia. If one meeting has a lot of believers in it, groups with fewer shouldn't feel they are part of a smaller Legislature, since both numbers combined equal the total number of believers in the city—the actual boundaries of the Legislature. In the next chapter I document many Scriptural examples of this lost truth.

In Acts, we also see that each city-wide, Legislature was given multiple leaders:

Acts 20:17-18, 28 (NKJ): [Paul] sent to Ephesus and called for the elders of the [Legislature]. And when they had come to him, he said to them...take heed to yourselves and to all the flock, among which the Holy Spirit has made you overseers, to shepherd the [Legislature] of God which He purchased with His own blood.

So in Ephesus, there was *one* Legislature (the word used here twice is singular) with *many* elders in it. And it was "God's Legislature," purchased by his blood, not belonging to any of the elders.

This fits completely with the rest of Scripture. The following all reveal plural human leadership in each of God's Legislatures of particular locations:

Acts 14:23 (NKJ): ...appointed *elders* in every church ["Legislature"]. (Notice that "Legislature" here is singular and "elders" is plural).

Phil 1:1 (NKJ): To all the saints in Christ Jesus who are in Philippi, with the [*overseers*] and [*servers*].

1 Thes 5:12 (NKJ): recognize *those* who labor among you, who [stand before you] in the Lord and admonish you...

Titus 1:5 (NKJ): ...appoint *elders* in every city...

Hebrews 13:7 (NASB): Remember *those* who [lead] you...imitate *their* faith.

Hebrews 13:17 (NASB): Obey your *leaders* and submit to *them*, for *they* keep watch over your souls as *those* who will give an account.

Hebrews 13:24 (NASB): Greet all of your *leaders*...

James 5:14 (NASB): ...call for the *elders* of the [Legislature].

1 Pet 5:1-2 (NASB): *Elders*...shepherd the flock among you...exercising oversight...

They had *one* Legislature per city with *many* leaders appointed by God to care for the individual believers. Plurality of human leaders is beneficial because each elder has different strengths. It also helps believers keep their eyes on Jesus. We need to come back to this plurality of leadership because it is the pattern God gave us in his Word, the only pattern he gave us. By obedience in this area, we'll discover by experience many other reasons why he did so.

We do typically have many leaders in each city today, but at this point they each operate by bringing together groups of believers and defining each group as a separate church. This is not accurate. Because of this, much needed networking and collaboration is not taking place between believers, including leaders, each in actuality part of the *same* Legislature in their city. In people's minds there is a distinction between the various groups of believers, which should not exist.

Today, there exist many organizations known as churches in a city, each under a different leader. A view that has emerged is that each group is a covering of protection for the believers who identify with it. The truth is that there is a protection of being in God's Legislature, but it is citywide and spiritual, not a mere human organization. You get in by being born again. You stay in by not being "handed over to Satan" (1Cor 5:5, 1Tim 1:20). You can participate in a variety of ways, as long as you're walking in the light.

The good news is you're covered by Jesus, the one Head

which the whole Legislature in your city is under. He justified you with his blood, and he also graciously provides leaders, for the Flock in your city, who are to personally train you in your walk and be available for you to call on in special times of need. They find you or you find them—as the Lord arranges.

The believers usually meet in smaller groups—in homes or in designated public places, as Acts 8:3 illustrates (quoted in the beginning of this chapter). Additionally, there are times when "*the whole* Legislature" in the city or town is involved in certain matters (See Ac 15:22).

While meeting in smaller groups, there's always to be a consciousness in everyone of belonging to the larger group, the Legislature in your city. According to Acts 15:22 and other Scriptures, the smaller groups are not whole "Churches" (unless they consist of all the believers in their city). They are parts of the one Legislature in a city. We must acknowledge, teach, and practice this lost truth, and walls will come down as a result.

Someone may say, "How can we all mix together and all be leaders of the same Church in our city? Who will be the leader?" The answer is Jesus Christ, the Head of his Body and Legislature. The result of dropping our names, divisions, denominations, etc. will be love, unity, and power like the world has never seen.

Part of our problem has been that we've viewed the boundaries of individual Legislatures as being the buildings they meet in—a traditional concept that began hundreds of years after Jesus ascended. But the original Legislature did not define itself or operate this way. Let's reform back to it.

Though in the New Testament we don't see groups of believers within cities having separate identities as "churches," we do see another picture. ☺. It's a scene of the various citywide Legislatures spurring each other on as they each advance spiritually. Here are some examples:

2 Cor 8:1-2, 7-8, 24 (NASB): Now, brethren, [writing to the Legislature in the city of Corinth] we wish to make known to you the grace of God which has been given in the [Legislatures] of [the province of] Macedonia, that in a

great ordeal of affliction their abundance of joy and their deep poverty overflowed in the wealth of their liberality...But just as you abound in everything...see that you abound in this gracious work also. I am not speaking this as a command, but as proving through the earnestness of others the sincerity of your love also...Therefore openly before the [Legislatures], show them the proof of your love and of our reason for boasting about you.

1 Thes 2:14 (NASB): For you, brethren, became imitators of the [Legislatures] of God in Christ Jesus that are in [the province of] Judea, for you also endured the same sufferings at the hands of your own countrymen, even as they did from the Jews.

IIThes 1:4 (NASB): [Addressing the Legislature in Thessalonica]: We ourselves speak proudly of you among the [Legislatures] of God for your perseverance and faith in the midst of all your persecutions and afflictions which you endure.

Phil 4:15 (NKJ): Now you Philippians know also that in the beginning of the gospel, when I departed from Macedonia, no [Legislature] shared with me concerning giving and receiving but you only.

Note that in the New Testament, the plural form of ekklesia, "*Legislatures*" ("Churches"), is always used in reference to *larger areas than cities*, such as provinces or states (I provide Scriptural examples in the next chapter).

Each city needs its own elders to oversee the flock living in it, and they have full authority from the Lord to do so. These elders and Legislatures are never to be considered lower or less legitimate than others outside, but to be under the Lord himself. Traveling ministers from more mature Legislatures may come and help, as we see in Acts, and healthy relationships can be made, but no Legislature is to be under any other, no matter how advanced one may be or seem.

This fact has very practical implications. Elders in a city do not need to look outside their city to other elders or organizations for a "covering." They've been "commended to the Lord" as their covering (Acts 14:23). When available, input from apostles and other servants is profitable and, at times, absolutely necessary. However, this is not always possible. When it's not, we can ask God for such help and patiently, confidently do what we can till he sends it. But we *don't* need to fear we're out of order or in rebellion.

I want to make this point again: elders in a city should *not* be "under" elders in another city, as if they are merely an extension of the Legislature of another city. They need to be governed by the Lord himself, if they have been appointed as elders through the Spirit. Otherwise, they won't depend fully on the Lord and receive his help. Once elders are in place, they need to look up to the Head and help younger believers learn to do the same. They also must remain open to help the Head sends through various ministries. There's an interdependence needed, rather than dependence or independence. And it's all under the Head, Jesus.

Chapter 17
Uses of Ekklesia in Scripture

A New Testament study of the singular form of Ekklesia, "a/the Legislature" is very eye-opening. In some cases, the term refers to all of God's People, and the boundaries include Heaven and Earth. Here are a few examples:

1. "On this rock I [King Jesus] will build my Legislature" (Mt 16:18)
2. "...the Anointed King is the Head of the Legislature..." (Eph 5:23)
3. "...He is the Head of the Body, the Legislature..." (Col 1:18)
4. "...the Legislature of the Firstborn, whose names are written in heaven" (Heb 12:23)

The other main use refers to a geographical location on Earth. Examining these reveals that the boundaries of "a Legislature" are synonymous with the political boundaries of the city or town where it is located. *The plural form of ekklesia ("churches") is never used when referring to one city.* Here are 25 examples of this usage:

1. "The Legislature which was at Jerusalem" (Ac 8:1)
2. "The Legislature in Jerusalem" (Ac 11:22)
3. "The Legislature" in Antioch (Ac 11:26)
4. "The Legislature that was at Antioch" (Ac 13:1)
5. "The Legislature" in Antioch (Ac 14:26-27)

6. "The Legislature" in Antioch (Ac 15:3)
7. "The Legislature" in Jerusalem (Ac 15:4)
8. "The whole Legislature" in Jerusalem (Ac 15:22)
9. "The Legislature" at Ceasarea (Ac 18:22)
10. "The Legislature" at Ephesus (Ac 20:17)
11. "The Legislature in Cenchrea" (Rom 16:1)
12. "The Legislature which is at Corinth" (1Cor. 1:2)
13. "The whole Legislature" in Corinth (1Cor. 14:23)
14. "The Legislature of God at Corinth" (2Cor. 1:1)
15. "The Legislature of the Laodiceans" (Col 4:16)
16. "The Legislature of the Thessalonians in God our Father…" (1Thes. 1:1)
17. "The Legislature of the Thessalonians in God our Father…" (2Thes. 1:1)
18. "The Legislature," at Ephesus (1Tim 5:16)
19. "The Legislature of Ephesus" (Rev 2:1)
20. "The Legislature of Smyrna" (Rev 2:8)
21. "The Legislature of Pergamos" (Rev 2:12)
22. "The Legislature of Thyatira" (Rev 2:18)
23. "The Legislature of Sardis" (Rev 3:1)
24. "The Legislature of Philadelphia" (Rev 3:7)
25. "The Legislature of the Laodiceans" (Rev 3:14)

There are more, but these 25 examples are sufficient to clearly establish that the boundaries of a Legislature are the city it's located in, just as the Greek and Roman governmental assemblies were one per city.

Understanding this, let's look at the uses of "Ekklesia" which refer to a Legislature in a house. There were three such houses mentioned:

1. The Legislature in Archippus' house (Phile 1:2)
2. The Legislature that is in Nymphas' house (Col 4:15)
3. The Legislature that is in Aquila and Priscilla's house (Rom 16:3-5, 1Cor. 16:19)

In light of the other clear uses, my conclusion is that these people, at that time, lived in cities that had just begun to be evangelized. In the beginning, as one house would be the only meeting place in a city, it would be the central location of that Legislature. Later, after the Lord added people to their number, they would need to meet in several houses, and the town's name would always be used to refer to its one Legislature.

A New Testament study of the plural form of Ekklesia, "Legislatures," reveals the same thing discovered above. The plural use of Ekklesia is always used when listing the existence of Legislatures in an area containing multiple cities, such as a province. The following 15 examples are just some of these uses:

1. Regarding Lystra, Iconium, and Antioch, reference to multiple Legislatures (Ac 8:1)
2. "The Legislatures throughout Judea, Galilee, and Samaria..." (Ac 9:31)
3. "[they] went through Syria and Cilicia, strengthening the Legislatures" (Ac 15:41)
4. "They went through the cities...so the Legislatures were strengthened" (Ac 16:4-5)
5. "All the Legislatures of the Gentiles" (in all locations outside Israel) (Rom 16:4)
6. "The Legislatures of Galatia" (1Cor 16:1)
7. "The Legislatures of Asia" (1Cor 16:19)
8. "The Legislatures of Macedonia" (2Cor 8:1)
9. "Other Legislatures" spoken of in contrast to the one in Corinth (2Cor 11:8)
10. "Other Legislatures" spoken of in contrast to the one in Corinth (2Cor 12:13)
11. "To the Legislatures of Galatia" (Gal 1:2)
12. "The Legislatures of Judea" (Gal 1:22)
13. Reference made to one Legislature in Philippi and to others in other places (Phil 4:15)
14. "The Legislatures of God which are in Judea in the Anointed King Jesus" (1Thes 2:14)
15. "To the seven Legislatures which are in Asia" (Rev 1:4)

In Scripture, the plural use of Ekklesia, "church*es*" ("Legislatures"), is not once used in reference to any one particular city. This knowledge can help us come back to the original understanding that each Legislature has as its boundaries the city in which it is located. Every believer in that city is part of it, by way of the new birth.

Chapter 18
The Unity of God's Legislatures

Paul worked very hard to keep believers in various Legislatures united. He plead with and had to rebuke the Legislature in Corinth for starting to divide:

1 Cor 1:10-13 (NKJ): Now I plead with you, brethren, by the name of our Lord Jesus Christ, that you all speak the same thing, and that there be no divisions among you, but that you be perfectly joined together in the same mind and in the same judgment. For it has been declared to me concerning you, my brethren...that there are contentions among you...that each of you says, "I am of Paul," or "I am of Apollos," or "I am of Cephas," or "I am of Christ." Is Christ divided? Was Paul crucified for you? Or were you baptized in the name of Paul?

1 Cor 3:3-5, 21-23 (NKJ): ...you are still carnal. For where there are envy, strife, and divisions among you, are you not carnal and behaving like mere men? For when one says, "I am of Paul," and another, "I am of Apollos," are you not carnal? Who then is Paul, and who is Apollos, but ministers [Gr., "servants"] through whom you believed, as the Lord gave to each one? Therefore let no one boast in men. For all things are yours: whether Paul or Apollos or Cephas, or the world or life or death, or things present or

things to come—all are yours. And you are Christ's, and Christ is God's.

The Word of God and every doctrine in it was given to all of us. Paul, Apollos, Peter, Luther, Wesley and every other servant of God and his People were gifts to all of us. We are not allowed by God to give ourselves a distinct identity from other parts of the Legislature based on leaders or particular doctrines. We will be tempted to do so, but it's immature. We need to resist that and choose to identify with the Body of Christ, not man-named organizations.

It's interesting that Paul faulted the person who said, "I am of Paul," *and* the person who said, "I am of Christ." The response to a person saying "I'm of Paul" shouldn't have been, "OK, well, I'm of Christ," but, "No! *We* are of Christ."

Lifting up the men and women God uses powerfully is the same as exalting dirt. God puts his New Covenant power in clay containers—the lowest type of container (2Cor 4:7). The greatest gifts he gives to the most deficient people, those who need such covering the most, because he cares for them (see 1Cor 12:23-25). Lifting them higher than oneself or others is like comparing one kind of dirt to another and praising the one. But the treasure inside, the new nature—we all have it in common. And God chooses to use the weak and lowly, the despised and the smallest, to bring forth his "strength" and silence Satan (Mt 21:16, Ps 8:2). He chooses weak things to shame the mighty (1Cor 1:27). We have to let him do so in and among us by not lifting up the dirt-jars he's already begun to show himself through. Christ in us should be the focus. His glory is infinite and available to come out of any of us—if we can keep our eyes on him.

Paul also said to the Corinthian Legislature, "no doubt there have to be *differences* among you" (1Cor 11:18-19). Differences are necessary and healthy since we're all different and growing. But *division* is not acceptable. We need to acknowledge our unity around Jesus being our Head and drop all potentially divisive, extra-Biblical, self-classification. Then, over time, our differences of doctrinal tradition and thinking will be worked out by the help of the Spirit of Truth himself, as long as we stay submitted to him and united in love (1Cor 11:19, Phil 3:15). We just need to keep unity of the Spirit through maintaining peace with each other and limiting our teaching to "speaking the truth in love." In this way, if a person departs from love, into contention or divisiveness, it will be apparent he's wrong, even to himself. Our differences will work for our good this way, as they will present opportunities to stay unified under Jesus the Head and essential truths. If we do this we'll grow tall together; we'll mature a lot. This kind of unity, around the Son of God, is a mark of our maturity (Eph 4:13).

Jesus is our Head. ☺.

Eph 1:22-23 (NKJ): And He [God] put all things under His [Jesus'] feet, and gave Him to be head over all things to the [Legislature], which is His body, the fullness of Him who fills all in all.

We're all in the same Body. We're unified, through the cross and the new birth. If we're alive to God, having been born-again, we're unified:

John 11:51-52 (NKJ): ...that Jesus would die for the nation [of Israel], and not for that nation only, but also that He would gather together *in one* the children of God who were scattered abroad.

Col 3:9-11 (NKJ): ...you have put off the old man with his deeds, and have put on the *new man* ["the Second Adam," "the New Creation"]...where there is neither Greek nor Jew, circumcised nor uncircumcised, barbarian, Scythian, slave nor free, but Christ is all and in all.

We haven't lived according to this truth only because we've let differences and personal preferences in our souls divide us, rather than living according to our New Creation, born again spirit. In light of our unity in Christ, described above, Paul immediately follows with this:

Col 3:12-15 (NKJ): Therefore, as the elect of God, holy and beloved, put on tender mercies, kindness, humility, meekness, longsuffering; bearing with one another, and forgiving one another, if anyone has a complaint against another; even as Christ forgave you, so you also must do. But above all these things put on love, which is the bond of perfection ["maturity"]. And let the peace of God [act as umpire] in your hearts, to which also you were called in *one body...*

Nowhere in the entire New Testament is any other head than Jesus described as given to the Legislature. He's the only one. The Legislature as a whole has only one (Eph 1:22-23, above); citywide Legislatures have only one (1Cor 12:21, 27; below); where two or three are gathered, the Head is also there (Mt 18:20); also each individual member has and must maintain his or her personal connection to the Head (Col 2:18-19).

As the Body, we all need each other:

1 Cor 12:21, 25 (NKJ): And the eye cannot say to the hand, "I have no need of you"; nor again the head to the feet, "I have no need of you"...that there should be no schism in the body, but that the members should have the same care for one another.

Notice here that even the Head (Jesus) can't say to the feet (the lowest members) that he doesn't need them. Dividing is self-destructive because the provision you need is in other parts of the Body, including those we don't esteem highly or which aren't "presentable" (1Cor 12:13-14). God set it up this way, and it won't change. He planned our success to exist through our unity and working together. To neglect it is to suffer. But to unify requires one major thing—self-humbling:

Eph 4:1-6 (NKJ): I, therefore, the prisoner of the Lord, beseech you to walk worthy of the calling with which you were called, with all lowliness and gentleness, with longsuffering, bearing with one another in love,

endeavoring to keep the unity of the Spirit in the bond of peace. There is one body and one Spirit, just as you were called in one hope of your calling; one Lord, one faith, one baptism; one God and Father of all, who is above all, and through all, and in you all.

If we walk according to the Gospel of the King, we will be united:

Phil 1:27 (NKJ): Only let your conduct be worthy of the gospel of Christ, so that whether I come and see you or am absent, I may hear of your affairs, that you stand fast in one spirit, with one mind striving together for the faith of the gospel.

I heard an illustration of the need for unity among God's People in a city. It was from a missionary to the native peoples of Mexico. As an apostle he goes into unreached areas. In one case, he founded a Legislature in a village, but over time two divided groups began to operate there. This apostle went to that village to bring healing to a severely sick woman among the believers. The person seemingly could not get healed, and it was puzzling to the brother. Then persecution hit all the believers in the village, and eventually the second group failed under the pressure. The believers from it who survived united with the first group. When they did, instantly the woman was healed.[14] The anointing flows through unity.

Ps 133 (NKJ): Behold, how good and how pleasant it is for brethren to dwell together in unity! It is like the precious oil upon the head, running down on the beard, the beard of Aaron, running down on the edge of his garments. It is like the dew of Hermon, descending upon the mountains of Zion; for there the LORD commanded the blessing— life forevermore.

---

[14] David Hogan of Freedom Ministries, *Fire of God 1 & 2*, MP3 Audio CDs.

John 17:20-23 (NKJ): I do not pray for these alone, but also for those who will believe in Me through their word; that they all may be one, as You, Father, are in Me, and I in You; that they also may be one in Us, that the world may believe that You sent Me. And the glory which You gave Me I have given them, that they may be one just as We are one: I in them, and You in Me; that they may be made perfect in one, and that the world may know that You have sent Me, and have loved them as You have loved Me.

John 13:34-35 (NKJ): A new commandment I give to you, that you love one another; as I have loved you, that you also love one another. By this all will know that you are My disciples, if you have love for one another."

If the believers in a city all drop their denominations and separations—our self-proclaimed and acknowledged divisions—and unify instead around Jesus, the simple Gospel and the Holy Spirit, the result will be the anointing mentioned in Psalm 133 on a citywide scale. If we drop our manmade foundations, we'll find ourselves on God's Foundation, Christ. Our disunity, one of the main accusations of the enemy against us, which keeps the world from accepting the Gospel, will be disarmed. And the believers will become an unstoppable force to bring the Gospel to their city and out beyond. Whole cities and eventually whole areas will be transformed.

Part 4: The Five Equipping-Ministries *& Beyond Them*

Ephesians 4:8, 11-16 (literal translation): ...When He [Jesus] ascended on high, he led captive a host of captives, and he gave gifts to men...He gave true apostles, and prophets, and evangelists, and shepherds, also[15] teachers, for the equipping of the saints for the work of service, to the building up of the body of Christ; until we all attain to the unity of the faith, and of the knowledge of the Son of God, to a mature man, to the measure of the stature which belongs to the fullness of Christ. That we no longer be children, tossed here and there by waves and carried about by every wind of doctrine, by the trickery of men, by craftiness in deceitful scheming; but speaking the truth in love, we are to grow up in all aspects into Him who is the head, Christ, from whom the whole body, being fitted and held together by the help of every joint, according to the proper working of each individual part, causes growth of the body for the building up of itself in love.

---

[15] This word, usually translated "and" here, is different than the "ands" proceeding it and is better translated "also." I believe teacher is separated out from the rest because it is often combined with other equipping gifts.

Chapter 19
Evangelism: the Way into the Legislature

The verb, "to evangelize," in Greek is "euaggelizo." It literally means to carry a message of good, or to bring good news. So evangelism literally means "carrying the Good News" to people. The verb is used of Jesus and others in the New Testament about 50 times. Usually it's translated "preach" or "preach the Gospel," though there are other Greek words also translated "preach." In the following Scriptures I've substituted "preach" for "evangelize" and/or "carry the Good News," according to the Greek:

Luke 4:18-19 (NKJ): "The Spirit of the Lord is upon Me, because He has anointed Me to *evangelize,* to *carry good news* to the poor; he has sent Me to heal the brokenhearted, to proclaim liberty to the captives and recovery of sight to the blind, to set at liberty those who are oppressed; to proclaim the acceptable year of the Lord."

Luke 9:1-2, 6 (NKJ): Then He called His twelve disciples together and gave them power and authority over all demons, and to cure diseases. He sent them to preach [Gr. here: "to proclaim," "to report"] the kingdom of God and to heal the sick...So they departed and went through the towns, *evangelizing/carrying the good news to people* and healing everywhere.

Luke 20:1 (NKJ): Now it happened on one of those days, as [Jesus] taught the people in the temple and *evangelized*...

Acts 8:4 (NKJ): ...those who were scattered went everywhere *evangelizing/carrying the good news to people.*

Acts 8:25 (NKJ): So when [Peter and John] had testified and preached [Gr. here: "uttered"] the word of the Lord, they returned to Jerusalem, *evangelizing* in many villages of the Samaritans.

Acts 16:10 (NKJ): Now after he had seen the vision, immediately we sought to go to Macedonia, concluding that the Lord had called us to *carry the good news* to them.

Rom 10:15 (NASB): How will they *carry the good news* unless they are sent? Just as it is written, "HOW BEAUTIFUL ARE THE FEET OF THOSE WHO BRING GOOD NEWS OF GOOD THINGS!"

Though in the beginning every believer evangelized, Philip is the clearest example of an *evangelist* we have in the Bible (Ac 8:5-40). We can understand the responsibilities of carrying the Good News through his work. When he went down to Samaria, he did the following four things:

1. Proclaimed the Good News of the Anointed King Jesus and God's Kingdom
2. Healed the sick and drove out demons (evidence and advertising of the first)
3. Baptized in water
4. Connected the new believers, as there was opportunity, to those who could oversee their growth

Proclaiming the simple Good News (1Cor 2:1-5) with the help of the Spirit (1Pe 1:12) allows the Lord to confirm it by signs, miracles, wonders, and gifts of the Spirit according to His will (Mk 16:20, Heb 2:4). People need to see a demonstration of God. It frees them from the domination of their five senses. They are humbled. They realize there really is a Power higher than them, and the foundation of feeling in control based on their five senses is broken. They get set free. They can reposition themselves on God. This will produce believers who really believe in God and revere him. It gives them a good start in going forward into a life of faith and radical change. This is an *essential* part of evangelism:

1 Cor 2:1-5 (NKJ): And I, brethren, when I came to you, did not come with excellence of speech or of wisdom declaring to you the testimony of God. For I determined not to know anything among you except Jesus Christ and Him crucified. I was with you in weakness, in fear, and in much trembling. And my speech and my preaching were not with persuasive words of human wisdom, but in demonstration of the Spirit and of power, that your faith should not be in the wisdom of men but in the power of God.

Healing was part of the original Good News, as was freedom from evil spirits. Jesus demonstrated this himself, and those he sent out did too. They all were commissioned to tell the Good News, heal, and drive out demons. In Acts, after Jesus ascended, they did the same according to Jesus' Great Commission:

Acts 14:7-10 (NKJ): And they were preaching the gospel [carrying the Good News to people] there. And in Lystra a certain man without strength in his feet was sitting, a cripple from his mother's womb, who had never walked. This man heard Paul speaking. Paul, observing him intently and seeing that he had faith to be healed, said with a loud voice, "Stand up straight on your feet!" And he

leaped and walked.

Where did this man get the faith Paul saw? "Faith comes by hearing..." (Rom 10:17). He heard Paul speaking Good News regarding healing. We have to get back to including this part of the Good News in our outreach.

Also we must keep in mind that the Gospel calls for a change in people's thinking. This is the literal meaning of the Greek word translated, "repent," which is "metanoeo" ("meta" means "change," and "noeo" is the *verb* form of "mind," in other words, "to think"). It means, "to change the way you think" or "to think differently," which will result in changing the way we live. The word's often been used incorrectly as a way to beat people down. We need to clearly understand that the word means, "change your way of thinking," that it's a gift (Ac 11:18, Ro 2:4, 2Tim 2:25) as well as a responsibility, and it's a requirement of being born again. Remember what Jesus said in the Great Commission: "that repentance [Gr., "changing the way one thinks"] unto forgiveness of sins should be proclaimed in his Name to all the nations" (Lk 24:46-49).

In other words, the Gospel brings people new information about life, God, and Jesus the risen King. Wholeheartedly accepting this information will result in a change, first in your thinking. To receive the forgiveness of sins, they have to believe this new information and acknowledge Jesus as Lord. It calls them to make a U-turn on their road of life, by the truth. They used to live for themselves. Now they live for the Lord. The true Gospel is radical and can't leave a person unchanged who accepts it.

Throughout our Christian lives our minds are to be renewed by the truth and our lifestyles changed. Changing our thinking ("repentance") is to be continual. But the initial truth people are to respond to is specifically regarding Jesus the King and God's authority (his Kingdom). We need to preach that Good News completely, which will bring people to a decision and powerfully help them. Then we are to baptize those who do believe. Those who respond to the Gospel by acknowledging Jesus as their Lord—their supreme Authority—won't have any problem obeying him in baptism.

Baptism in water follows believing. This was instituted by the Lord as a powerful first step of faith into discipleship. It was commanded to be done as soon as possible after a person verbally accepted the message (Ac 10:48). This separated out those who were serious from those who were not. It's very important that this be restored to modern Christianity. The Scriptural way of calling for new converts after proclaiming the Good News includes baptism in water (Ac 2:37-38, Ac 22:16).

There was little or no delay in baptizing new converts in early evangelism. It gave an experiential point of initiation into Christianity. It also visually reinforced, for those already on their path of discipleship, the truth of our identification with Christ (Rom 6:1-11)—our death, burial and resurrection with him, and all that follows. In the Book of Acts, no believer is mentioned who didn't receive baptism in water.

Baptism in water is one of the few physical rituals given us in the New Covenant (others being The Lord's Meal, laying on of hands, and anointing with oil). Because of its importance, it's been attacked constantly by Satan over the centuries. However, we will beat him if we simply reform to the original way.

The Greek word, "baptizo," simply and clearly means, "<u>to immerse</u>." It was unfortunately *transliterated* into English as "baptism," according to the Greek word's pronunciation. This is a historical example of a transliteration done for the purpose of concealing the meaning of the original word. Because the Church of England was practicing the tradition of sprinkling babies at the time, the KJV translators did not translate the word, "immersion," but created a new English word, "baptism," out of the Greek, "baptizo." This has caused much confusion, ignorance, and even division in the Legislature. It's also caused us to often fail to carry out King Jesus' command. So we must all get back to the Bible's definition and practice of immersion.

Acts records that Philip "preached Jesus" to the Ethiopian eunuch (Acts 8:35). The next verse describes the Eunuch requesting immersion in the water alongside the road. How did he know to request it? Because it was part of Philip's message. 'See that?

The statements in the New Testament regarding water immersion are so strong that Protestants often shy away from them. The Protestant movement so strongly contended for the truth of "justification by faith" that Protestants have a tendency to see some Bible verses as a threat or contradictory to it. But they are not. We need to accept the whole Bible and let the Spirit sort it all out for us. We shouldn't neglect any part—they all fit together. Most of us from Protestant backgrounds today wouldn't dare use language used in the New Testament in reference to water immersion. The Lord and his early disciples simply didn't have the theological hang-ups we do. Take a look at some of their statements:

Mark 16:16 (NASB): He who believes and is baptized will be saved; but he who does not believe will be condemned.

Acts 2:38 (NASB): Then Peter said to them, "[Change your thinking], and let every one of you be baptized in the name of Jesus Christ for the remission of sins..."

Acts 22:16 (NASB): [Spoken by Ananias to Saul] And now why are you waiting? Arise and be baptized, and wash away your sins, calling on the name of the Lord.

1 Pet 3:21 (NASB): Corresponding to that, baptism now saves you—not the removal of dirt from the flesh, but an appeal to God for a good conscience—through the resurrection of Jesus Christ.

What they said was the truth. It's we who need to adjust. We need to hold all truths simultaneously. There is no contradiction. Actually, neglecting verses in the Bible leaves room for cults to form. They take pride in believing the neglected truths of the majority of true believers. Then they make more out of those truths than was originally intended and attempt to legitimize their organizations by doing so.

In Romans 10, Paul states what is specifically needed to be "saved" (speaking of the salvation of the spirit, being born again). He says people must hear the Good News communicated, so they can believe. Then they can acknowledge Jesus as the risen Lord, the "Authority" they will yield to from then on, call on him to save them, and he will absolutely do so. This is also what we see in Acts, and immersion always immediately followed.

In order to restore the lost *importance* and *urgency* of immersion in water, I list several more verses below. I've substituted "baptized" with "immersed," according to the original meaning. These bring us back to the practice of the Book of Acts, God's pattern for us:

Acts 2:41 (NKJ): Then those who gladly received his word were *immersed*; and that day about three thousand souls were added to them.

Acts 8:12 (NKJ): But when they believed Philip as he preached the things concerning the kingdom of God and the name of Jesus Christ, both men and women were *immersed*.

Acts 10:48 (NKJ): Can any man forbid water, that these should not be *immersed*?...And he commanded them to be *immersed* in the name of the Lord. Then they asked him to stay a few days.

Acts 16:14-15 (NKJ): Now a certain woman named Lydia heard us...The Lord opened her heart to heed the things spoken by Paul. And when she and her household were *immersed*...

Acts 16:33-34 (NKJ): And he took them the same hour of the night and washed their stripes. And immediately he and all his family were *immersed*. Now when he had brought them into his house, he set food before them; and he rejoiced, having believed in God with all his household.

Acts 18:8 (NKJ): Then Crispus, the ruler of the synagogue,

believed on the Lord with all his household. And many of the Corinthians, hearing, believed and were *immersed*.[16]

We see from these verses, and there are more, that every believer was immersed in water—and there was *no delay*. It's always to be done at the point of sincerely receiving the Gospel.

The first verse I listed above, Acts 2:41, states that those who "gladly received" the message were immersed in water. Those who gladly receive the full message today will also be immersed when instructed to. We don't need to fear that it's too strong of a commitment. In those days they didn't have the many bathtubs and other facilities we do today, so it was less convenient for them. But they were immersed in obedience to the directives from the Lord's own mouth before he ascended.

In 1Peter 3:20-21, Peter identifies the passing of Noah's family through the flood in the ark as a prefiguring of immersion in water. One reason for the flood and Noah's Ark was to provide a picture of immersion for us today (Rom 15:4). In the Ark they passed through water, out of one world and into a new one. They left behind a rebellious social order and entered, through water, into one in which God was worshiped and everything could grow and be established anew. This happens now when believers get immersed in water in the Name of Jesus.

In 1Corinthians 10:1-2, Paul shows another prefigure of immersion in water. He says that the Israelites, first redeemed from Egypt by the Passover Lamb's blood, were also all "immersed into Moses, in the cloud and in the sea." Then he goes on to list other aspects of their experience that relate to our lives now. Immersion in the cloud represents immersion in the Holy Spirit. Immersion in the sea represents water immersion. Both were, "into Moses," (Moses being a prefigure of Christ, Ac 7:37). We need to know that the Israelites were

---

[16] Note: from 1Cor 1:13-17 we learn that Paul personally immersed Crispus, but most of those mentioned here were immersed by others. Paul also had to correct the Corinthians' thinking, telling them the one who does the immersing is not important at all, nor is it done in his or her name, nor in the name of a human organization, but in the Name/Authority of King Jesus.

redeemed, not by passing through the Red Sea, but by the blood of the Passover Lamb applied to their households. Passing through the water facilitated their transition out of Egypt (a figure of the world) where they had been slaves under Pharaoh (a figure of Satan), and into a life of faith, worship, and hope in the desert (a prefigure of life in the Legislature during this age, accompanied by the Holy Spirit and on our journey to our promised inheritance in God's Kingdom).

If we don't baptize those who gladly receive our message, we are not only missing the mark on what Jesus commanded and the early disciples exemplified, we're also denying new converts a blessing that comes, every time, in response to their obedience to be immersed. And we're weakening the divide between the old life and the new Life.

We also need to recognize God's <u>initiation process into Christianity</u> for new converts. It starts with evangelists. Often new believers today do not receive the four provisions listed earlier, which God and Philip provided them. Again, Philip

1. Proclaimed the Good News of the Anointed King Jesus and the Kingdom of God
2. Healed the sick and drove out demons (evidence and advertising of the first)
3. Immersed in water
4. Connected the new believers, as there was opportunity, to those who could oversee their growth

Had Philip left too early, the survival of the new converts would have been slimmer. The work of those who cared for them afterward would have been harder also.

This implicates great reform of the work of evangelists today. In most cases, they cannot just help people receive the new birth and move on. They need to provide all of these they can, by faith and in pace with the Spirit.

An illustration of this need is found in the way Jesus raised Lazarus from the dead in John 11. First, he had people role away the stone. He needed their help. This represents evangelism. Then, he did his job—he raised Lazarus from the dead. Lastly, he ordered those helping him to take off the grave clothes and let him go. When we are spiritually raised from the dead, born-again, we come out with a bunch of grave-clothes wrapped all around our bodies and heads. There's a lot of work needed at that point from others. It's not Jesus' job to do all of that through the new birth. It's his helpers' job.

On a final note, Philip called down two apostles, Peter and John, and handed the new believers off to them. If there had been elders already in Samaria, it's apparent that Philip would've connected the believers to them instead. But in this case, Philip connected them to apostles to work with them further and eventually appoint elders. These elders would shepherd and oversee the Legislature there, ensuring it evangelized the rest of Samaria and grew to maturity. Eventually, it would send out apostles and other servants as called for by the Holy Spirit, according to the goal of completing the Great Commission.

Chapter 20
Teachers, Prophets, and Shepherding

As mentioned in the last chapter, the initiation process into Christianity is *started by evangelism*. To the extent they can, evangelists, or whoever brought the Gospel, should work with new converts till they have received each of the four evangelistic provisions Philip gave that they need. This is extremely important. It's like cleaning up a baby right after it's born, cutting the umbilical cord, preparing it for life in this world. No matter our skill level, we should seek to provide those things and seek help when needed. The last of them was introducing new converts to overseers, or a more mature disciple if need be, who can shepherd them and oversee their growth.

Once new believers are in the hands of good oversight they also need the help of teachers and prophets. The three provisions of shepherding, teaching, and prophecy work very well together to help believers develop a solid walk with the Lord.

Therefore, the second part of the initiation process into Christianity is generally to be provided *by overseers and shepherds, teachers, and prophets*. Elders, as part of their shepherding function, care for sheep, making sure they are eating, digesting, moving forward, and accounted for. The equipping gift of shepherds does so also. Note: these generally *do not* need to grow the food. That's mainly the job of teachers, or, farmers, in the physical world, rather than sheep-herders. So elders or shepherds work with teachers to provide the food required for believers to grow. They may take the sheep to where the food is or bring the food to where the sheep are, either way.

Again, elders oversee and shepherd the sheep where they live. They watch to be sure they are continuing sincerely on their journey toward the Kingdom, protected, being fed, and doing their ministries. Teachers grow the food for the sheep. Elders and shepherds help sheep hold on to and apply good teaching. Teachers also impart a love for the Word of God and an example so that all believers can better teach one another.

Teachers can be utilized at all points in a disciple's life, but I want to emphasize that it is very important for new disciples to be connected to good teaching right away as part of their initiation into Christianity.

In Acts, when people first came to the Lord, two major changes to their lifestyle were particularly explained to all of them early on. They were instructed to abstain from anything to do with both sexual immorality and the occult (idolatry, witchcraft, spiritual magic, etc.). These likewise need to be explained to all new believers today, so they may, "do well" in their new Life (see Ac 15:28-31 & 16:4-5). These are two things we're specifically commanded to flee from (1Cor 6:18, 10:14).

Additionally, there are several foundational teachings that will help new believers grow successfully. These make up a foundation for believers' faith. Building it takes a good amount of time and the combined work of teachers and overseers, among others.

Hebrews 6:1-2 lists the "elementary teachings of the Anointed King," a foundation that was laid for the believers in Jerusalem. It lists the following five points, which can provide a great outline for the second part of the initiation process into Christianity:

1. Repentance—changing the way we think and live, in response to the Truth of God we hear
2. Faith—walking by God's Word, regardless of physical senses; utilizing the faith of God through the Spirit, etc.

3. Immersions—the two main ones in the Bible are in water and in the Spirit
4. Laying on of hands—for healing and for commissioning
5. Resurrection of the dead and eternal judgment —including the first and second resurrections, the Judgment throne of Christ, and the Great White Throne judgment

Many believers who've attended Sunday morning meetings for many years still don't have much of a foundation of the basic truths of the New Testament in their hearts. This can be discovered by simply talking with them, asking questions. If the facilitators of a group put out a survey among attendees, they will very likely be *shocked* by their findings.

Evangelists and overseers (as well as shepherds) need to swap contact information. So should shepherds, teachers, and prophets. They should all stay in touch and work together to make sure every sincere believer in their city reaches maturity. Overseers and shepherds can introduce people to good teaching by distributing materials and hosting events in which teachers come in and teach. They can also endorse the ongoing work of teachers in a city or facilitate such ongoing teaching if none currently exists. There will be a need for much, much more teaching than 1 hour per week on Sunday, and it must be ongoing and with a great variety to meet people where they are in life.

In addition to the foundational doctrines listed above, these topics were all fundamental to early Legislatures:

6. Everything in the first four Gospels (Mt 7:24-27, 28:20)
7. Jesus as Messiah, Lord, and Savior (Rom 10:9)
8. God as Father (Jn 17:6)
9. The Spirit as our Helper; the Law of the Spirit (Jn 14:16)
10. Forgiveness and redemption through the blood of Jesus and our responsibility to forgive others (Mt 6:12, 18:35)
11. Freedom from this age, this world, sin, the Old Man, etc (Ro 6-8, Galatians, James 1)
12. The Lord's return and the hope of the Gospel, foundational to a life of faith and love (Col 1:5-7)

13. The fact that we will suffer, in addition to the blessings we receive as disciples (1Thes 3:3-4, Mk 10:29-30, Jn 15:18-20, Rev 1:9)
14. Righteousness by faith (Rom 3, 5)
15. Strength through faith (Rom 4, Col 2:7)
16. Freedom from sin and the flesh (Rom 6)
17. Freedom from the law (Rom 7)
18. The new law (Rom 8)
19. Love for one another (1Jn 3:11)
20. Distinctiveness (i.e., "holiness") from the world system and the call to be made increasingly distinct in purity, love, thankfulness, etc., (1Thes 4:1-3)
21. Sexual purity/God's esteem of and provision of Marriage (1Thes 4:1-3, Ac 15:28-31, 16:4-5, 1Cor 7)
22. Keeping away from idolatry/the occult (Ac 15:28-31, 16:4-5, 1Jn 5:21)
23. Caring for the poor (Jas 1:27)
24. God's Kingdom in a family/his order for the family (in several epistles of the NT, so vital)
25. Spiritual gifts—considered spiritual "milk" (1Cor 12:1, 4-11)
26. The fruit of the Spirit (Gal 5:22-24)
27. Praise, thanksgiving, worship, financial giving (various)
28. Our kingly authority, on the throne with Jesus (Eph 1:19-23)
29. The nature of the spiritual battle we're in (Eph 6:12-18)
30. Relating well to human governments (1Pe 2:13-17, Rom 13:1-8, Jn 19:10-11, 1Tim 2:1-4)
31. God's purposes for Israel—distinct from the Legislature, his future plan for that special nation, and the attitude believers must maintain toward it (Rom 11:17-19)
32. The Great Mystery, or "Secret"—for the mature (1Cor 2:6-7, Mt 13, Eph 3:3-6)
33. The Lord's Body, the Legislature—as we're discussing

To cover a topic, a teacher may need to spend many hours on it. If the only format for teaching is an hour a week on Sunday mornings, these truths will be taught too slowly. However, classes, books, multi-media, and different meeting formats, in public and in homes, are other ways to facilitate

Gospel teaching.

I sat through a class once on the Holy Spirit and exercising our spiritual authority. The teacher taught for about 28 hours on the subject in 6 days time. Of course, we needed to keep studying and applying the material for years to get it deep into our hearts. But this 28 hours in one week amounts to over six months of teaching at the pace of one hour per week on Sunday mornings! And it was life-changing. Teachers often need a format that includes several hours at a time to teach. With modern technology, their teaching can be captured on video and audio and received by believers outside of meetings also.

Prophets are messengers whose ministry is to deliver "the word of the Lord," a specific message suited for God's People at the right time. One aspect of their work is to speak God's future plan, helping groups and individuals to see it in order to reach it (Ac 3:24, 11:27). Another aspect is to bring correction and help people stay on track or get back on track if they've strayed. They may need to call God's People back to the Truth. They may exhort and confirm God's People (Ac 15:32). They often work among believers in a city (Ac 13:1) or alongside apostles as they travel and lay the foundation for Legislatures (Eph 2:20, Ac 15:32, 40). They may come alongside believers and pass on messages they receive from God—not always grand ones, but what is actually needed at the time. They can also be great examples for other disciples since all New Covenant believers can prophesy (Ac 2:17-18, 1Cor 14:31).

Elders mainly care for people; teachers and prophets mainly care for the Words of God. If disciples exclusively hear teachers, they may become overly knowledge-based. Prophets help keep things dynamically moving. With continual teaching but no prophecy, disciples can become comfortable just learning many wonderful truths but not receiving specific attention from the Father and not having their lives shaken up. Prophecy can shake God's People's worlds up, through the future realities it may bring out. Through the prophetic ministry, God can set a believer on a course such as Joseph's, through a prison into a palace.

Elders and shepherds make sure truths are really

understood and lived out by the sheep. The shepherding ministry is down to earth, up close and personal. It requires examining, listening, supporting and guiding. With continual teaching but no shepherding, believers often get into a rut of hearing over and over but not doing, a typical problem of our current structure.

As the Legislature grows up, through the influence of these gifts and others, and through the whole Body speaking the truth in love to each other, some disciples will emerge qualified to be appointed by the Spirit as apostles. They will extend the Kingdom outward, beyond its current boundaries.

Chapter 21
Understanding the Work of Apostles

Let's look at some basics regarding apostles. The word in Greek translated "apostle" is "apostolos," which means literally, "a person set apart and sent away." This meaning of the word itself gives insight into this office, and we learn more about it from Scriptural statements and examples.

Jesus sent out the first twelve apostles. He "set them apart" out of a larger group of disciples ("students"), by the will of God revealed to him.

Luke 6:12-13 (NKJ): Now it came to pass in those days that He went out to the mountain to pray, and continued all night in prayer to God. And when it was day, He called His disciples to Himself; and from them He chose twelve whom He also named apostles.

What made these twelve distinct from the other disciples was their special task of being sent out:

Matt 10:1-2,5 (NKJ): And when He had called His twelve disciples to Him, He gave them power over unclean spirits, to cast them out, and to heal all kinds of sickness and all kinds of disease. Now the names of the twelve apostles are these...These twelve Jesus sent out...

This aspect of their calling—being set apart and sent forth—is basic and fundamental. The first twelve, and others later, were called apostles in conjunction with actually being sent out. Note also that the lifestyle of true apostles is very difficult:

1 Cor 4:9-14 (NKJ): For I think that God has displayed us, the apostles, last, as men condemned to death; for we have been made a spectacle to the world, both to angels and to men. We are fools for Christ's sake, but you are wise in Christ! We are weak, but you are strong! You are distinguished, but we are dishonored! To the present hour we both hunger and thirst, and we are poorly clothed, and beaten, and homeless. And we labor, working with our own hands. Being reviled, we bless; being persecuted, we endure; being defamed, we entreat. We have been made as the filth of the world, the offscouring of all things until now. I do not write these things to shame you, but as my beloved children I warn you.

The initial twelve apostles were set apart before Jesus' resurrection. Afterward, the Scripture states that "he also gave true apostles..." (Eph 4:11, lit.). So there have been additional apostles given by the Lord since his ascension. In the New Testament, there are twenty-eight people specifically referred to as apostles. The translators of the Bible into English sometimes translated "apostolos" incorrectly, but a careful study of the Greek New Testament uses of "apostolos" makes this number unquestionably clear.[17]

How were the apostles commissioned after Jesus ascended? By the Holy Spirit he sent to us. We can see from the examples of Paul and Barnabas, both apostles (Ac 14:14), that the calling comes from Heaven:

Gal 1:1 (NKJ): Paul, an apostle (not from men nor through man, but through Jesus Christ and God the Father who raised Him from the dead).

---

[17] Derek Prince, *The Church—Vo. 1—Universal & Local* (Charlotte, NC: Derek Prince Ministries, 2004), Audio CD#5003; Derek Prince, *Rediscovering God's Church* (New Kinsington, PA: Whitaker House, 2006), 218.

It does *not* originate in the minds of men, but in the mind of God and the Lord Jesus the King. Then the Holy Spirit, on Earth, tells some disciples to separate out of their group those who will be sent away as apostles:

Acts 13:2-4 (NKJ): As they [a group of disciples from the Legislature in Antioch] ministered to the Lord and fasted, the Holy Spirit said, "Now separate to Me Barnabas and Saul for the work to which I have called them." Then, having fasted and prayed, and laid hands on them, they sent them away. So, being sent out by the Holy Spirit, they went down to Seleucia...

They were called before this event happened, and they must have had at least some knowledge of this calling in their own spirits. But they became apostles at this time, as the Legislature cooperated with the Holy Spirit in sending them out. From then on they were apostles and referred to as such in Acts.

So what was this work they were called and sent out to do as apostles? Disciples with various ministries were "sent off" by Legislatures in Acts to do various things, but not all were called apostles (E.g., Ac 15:32-33). It's not just being sent out that makes a person an apostle, though that's fundamental. What did these apostles do when they were sent out? First of all, they evangelized (see Ac chp. 13-14; 1Thes 1:1, 2:6; 2Tim 4:5). But they did more than Philip did. They also laid the Foundation among believers:

1 Cor 3:10-11 (NKJ): According to the grace of God which was given to me, as a wise master builder I have laid the foundation...which is Jesus Christ.

This took time and labor among them. It meant caring for the new believers deeply, as parents in the faith (1Cor 4:14-16, Gal 4:19, 1Jn 2:1, 3Jn vs. 4):

1 Thes 2:7, 10-11 (NKJ): ...we were gentle among you, just

as a nursing mother cherishes her own children...You are witnesses, and God also, how devoutly and justly and blamelessly we behaved ourselves among you who believe; as you know how we exhorted, and comforted, and charged every one of you, as a father does his own children...

Acts 20:31 (NKJ): Therefore watch, and remember that for three years I did not cease to warn everyone night and day with tears.

Eventually they appointed elders by the Spirit (Ac 14:23). This was all part of founding Legislatures. Paul said to Titus, who seems to be a young apostle he was mentoring:

Titus 1:5 (NKJ): For this reason I left you in Crete, that you should set in order the things that are lacking [NIV: "the things left unfinished"], and appoint elders in every city as I commanded you...

At one time, Paul called the Legislature he founded in Corinth his seal of apostleship:

1 Cor 9:2 (NKJ): If I am not an apostle to others, yet doubtless I am to you. For you are the seal of my apostleship in the Lord.

A seal is the public evidence of authenticity. It was used extensively in the ancient world, and, in various forms, is still used today. If anyone questioned Paul's apostleship, he could say, "Go to Corinth; look at the Legislature there. I founded it on Jesus Christ. Ask them. You'll know I'm an apostle."

After Legislatures had elders, apostles continued to serve them (e.g., Phil 1:1). Apostles have a much longer-term vision for disciples than evangelists, in addition to the vision to evangelize. Timothy and Titus provided ongoing service to Legislatures after elders had been appointed. Paul never went to Colossae, but he gave help to the Legislature there, which was evangelized by his co-worker Epaphras and seemed to be doing well (Col 1:6-8). Peter worked in Corinth after Paul had founded the Legislature there (1Cor 3:12, 22). Paul served the Legislature in Rome, even after they were quite mature (Rom 15:14-16). Paul and Barnabas remained in Antioch at one point in order to teach and evangelize alongside many other disciples (Ac 15:35). And we learn from Peter's statement about himself that in evangelized areas, apostles are "co-elders" or "associate elders" alongside elders (1Pe 5:1).

The ministry of apostle carries with it authority to discipline (see 1Cor 5:3-4; 2Cor 2:5-11, 13:10; 1Tim 1:20; Gal 5:10, 6:1; 3Jn vs. 9-10; Ac 5:1-9). This must sometimes be used to publically correct elders, if they are persisting in sin. If no apostles are present, it would be fitting that other elders in the city carry out this solemn responsibility:

1 Tim 5:19-21 (NASB): Do not receive an accusation against an elder except on the basis of two or three witnesses. Those who continue in sin, rebuke in the presence of all, so that the rest also will be fearful of sinning. I solemnly charge you in the presence of God and of Christ Jesus and of His chosen angels, to maintain these principles without bias, doing nothing in a spirit of partiality.

Another characteristic of apostles is that they continue to go. As long as they are functioning as apostles, they will desire to go further, till the work is done. If they don't have that drive, the world won't be reached. But God put it in them. They can build on foundations other apostles have laid, and they do work alongside elders at times, but they're not satisfied with that. Paul expressed his apostolic drive this way:

Rom 15:20-21 (NKJ): ...I have made it my aim to preach the gospel, not where Christ was named, lest I should build on another man's foundation, but as it is written: "To whom He was not announced, they shall see; and those who have not heard shall understand."

Finally, apostles should remember the poor. This next verse places caring for the needy alongside apostolic work:

Gal 2:9-10 (NKJ): ...James, Cephas, and John...gave me and Barnabas the right hand of fellowship, that we should go to the Gentiles and they to the circumcised. They desired only that we should remember the poor, the very thing which I [Paul] also was eager to do.

In Paul's last words to the elders of Ephesus, he instructed them to care for the needy. This emphasis was one of the main things he wanted them to receive from him:

Acts 20:33-35 (NKJ): I have coveted no one's silver or gold or apparel. Yes, you yourselves know that these hands have provided for my necessities, and for those who were with me. I have shown you in every way, by laboring like this, that you must support the weak. And remember the words of the Lord Jesus, that He said, "It is more blessed to give than to receive."

Elsewhere, Paul instructed all believers along these lines:

Gal 6:10 (NKJ): ...as we have opportunity, let us do good to all, especially to those who are of the household of faith.

So to summarize, apostles are sent out by the Spirit to:

1. Evangelize
2. Found Legislatures on Jesus Christ in unreached villages/towns/cities
3. Appoint elders to shepherd and oversee the flock
4. Provide ongoing support, at times, for Legislatures, including teaching, correction and discipline when needed
5. Continue to extend the boundaries of the Kingdom of God
6. Care for the poor and inspire others to do the same

All apostles must be tested. Jesus commends those who do so:

Rev 2:2 (NIV): I know your deeds, your hard work and your perseverance. I know that you cannot tolerate wicked people, that you have tested those who claim to be apostles but are not, and have found them false.

We shouldn't be intimidated out of testing or feel it not necessary because a certain apostle is or seems so wonderful. They're all fallible; they can be wrong. We must love them and test them. One true apostle who was sent out by Jesus while on Earth changed and became false (Judas), another made some serious mistakes at times (Peter).

Also, it's not that uncommon nowadays to meet people who had the role of "senior pastor" for many years, enjoyed the preeminence they got out of that, and when the new popular title of "apostle" came around, they switched over to it. But their lifestyle may be nothing like what the Scripture reveals about apostles.

We've looked at the calling, commissioning and work of apostles, and the seal of apostleship—an established Legislature. There are also *signs* of apostles:

2 Cor 12:12 (NASB): The signs of a true apostle were performed among you [in] all perseverance, by signs and wonders and miracles.

The signs of an apostle listed here are miraculous signs, wonders, and miracles, with great perseverance.

Chapter 22
Restoring the Gift of Shepherds

Jesus is called "the Apostle" we confess (Heb 3:1), the "One...Teacher" (Mt 23:10), "the Prophet" (Jn 6:14), and though he's not specifically called "the Evangelist/Herald," he is said many times to "evangelize," (usually translated "preach the Gospel"). His work in Israel included evangelizing continually (Lk 4:43-44); he's the model Evangelist. However, in Scripture Jesus was called "the Shepherd" most of all. This aspect of his ministry is particularly special. Here are just some of his titles relating to his ministry as our Shepherd:

- The Good Shepherd (Jn 10:11)
- The One Shepherd (Jn 10:16)
- The Shepherd struck by God (Mt 26:31)
- That Great Shepherd (Heb 13:20)
- The Shepherd and Overseer of our souls (1Pe 2:25)
- The Chief Shepherd, or "Head Shepherd/Lead Shepherd" (1Pe 5:4)

Jesus is my Shepherd. He is one of a kind.

At times, I also need human shepherds appointed by Jesus to watch over my growth and help me reach the destination of reigning with him in the next age.

Though a portion of Jesus' shepherding ministry is entrusted to leaders and to shepherds, they are *never* meant to replace him. Regardless of current leadership, all believers should have in their hearts at all times that Jesus is their

Shepherd, first and foremost. To the extent that a human is estimated by a believer to be his or her shepherd more so than the Lord himself, the system has failed—no matter how gifted the human shepherd. It's become unhealthy.

Have you ever heard anyone say, "Jesus is my Pastor"? It almost sounds like heresy or rebellion to many of us. And, yet, looking at the Bible we can see that in the early Legislature for someone to say one man was his or her shepherd would sound like heresy. They saw Jesus as their Shepherd first. Then they saw the men—who were feeble, weak, but doing the best they could and qualified and empowered by the Holy Spirit to perform their high calling—they saw them as a necessary provision also to make it on their journey.

Early Legislatures had many shepherds, many teachers, and others. But only One was, "the Shepherd" or "my Shepherd." I believe reference to "*the* shepherd" or "*the* prophet" or whatever ministry there is should generally be reserved for the Lord Jesus.

The Scripture states very clearly, both in 1Timothy 3:1 and in Titus 1:6, that "anyone" can be an elder. It's a position of leadership among God's People, just as "elder" equaled "leader" in Israel and virtually the entire ancient world. Those who desired the leadership position of elder were allowed to test for it (1Tim 3:1-2). On the other hand, the gift of shepherd is something restricted only to those given it by the Lord (Eph 4:8-11)—it's not available to "anyone." For this reason, I believe Scripture reveals clearly that the gift of shepherd is distinct from the leadership role of elder/overseer.

Shepherding implies leading and guiding the sheep, watching out for them, feeding them, protecting them from wolves or going astray, fleecing them, possibly cleaning them from lice or tics, or helping them recover from a wound or disease.

Shepherding also includes bringing stray sheep into the fold and going after lost ones (Lk 15:3-7). A shepherd is attracted to a sheep that needs his help, similarly to the way evangelists are sometimes attracted to specific unbelievers who need to hear the Good News. He uses his shepherd's crook to guide them into the fold—into a place where they can get good teaching and grow in healthy relationships with other believers.

Jesus is the Good Shepherd who leaves the 99 to search for the one lost sheep (Lk 15:1-7). As he is in Heaven now, he must do this through us, his Body. This is part of why he gave shepherds, to help him seek and rescue straying believers.

Shepherding also includes *feeding* sheep. According to 1Timothy 5:17, elders are not necessarily teachers, though they shepherd. Shepherding does not require *growing* the food. Shepherds take the sheep to good food or bring good food to the sheep. They seek to distinguish the true and profitable teaching from the unprofitable and harmful. If an elder or a shepherd is gifted as a teacher, he or she may also "labor in Word" (1Tim 5:17), but this is not a main function of *shepherding*.

True shepherds will have in them a desire to see believers benefit from the Word they hear. They don't feel they must be the ones teaching it. They may naturally give out good teaching to believers—in the form of books, audio messages, etc., similar to the way evangelists may give out Gospel literature. They have a real heart to see other believers grow and stay on track on their journey.

Physical shepherds help sheep eat food. They sometimes have to physically help them get the food down through their mouths. This is also the work of spiritual shepherds. Sheep will hear teaching but often need help applying it to their lives. The truth doesn't necessarily click or stick in them. So Jesus gave the responsibility of shepherding to his leaders to help his sheep process and utilize the Words he sends them, and stay on track by them.

Now let's consider oversight. Oversight is for the most part a lost spiritual art among us. It requires a "hands off" approach to individuals, long enough to see where they are. In a hospital, to check a patient's condition a doctor may check his tongue. Overseers do the same with saints who need it. They hear what they say, and they also see what they do, until they can identify where they are and what they may need at that time, if anything. This kind of sight requires time with people. It requires listening to them.

This is very different than the hands-on, teaching ministry. If teachers aren't doing anything, they aren't fulfilling their ministry. They have to teach. They have to give something. But after shepherds get sheep up and moving, they only need to watch, and then help as needed.

Perhaps a more modern and fitting translation than "overseer" is "supervisor." Supervisors don't *do* all the work; they watch to make sure the work is being done. They're not in the spotlight, doing all the ministering. Rather, they help ensure everyone else fulfills their ministries.

Oversight implies standing guard over God's property, watching to make sure everything is moving forward in people's faith and walk. It's a quiet job. Physical shepherds do this with their flocks.

The teaching of the Word is an awesome thing. However young believers need oversight so they don't lose the Words entrusted to them and aren't destroyed by the enemy. This is *severely* lacking in our current form; it basically doesn't exist, apart from a few isolated cases. Consequently, without a shepherd, the sheep are scattered, harassed, helpless (see Ezek 34:5, Matt 9:36). It's an onslaught out there. And more or better teaching alone won't solve the problem.

Another lost aspect of shepherding to be recovered is going to people where they are:

Jer 23:2-3 (NKJ): Therefore thus says the Lord God of Israel against the shepherds who feed My people: "You have scattered My flock, driven them away, and not attended to [Heb., "visited"] them. Behold, I will attend to ["visit"] you for the evil of your doings," says the Lord.

The literal Hebrew for what these shepherds should have done here is "visited," as I've noted above (the KJV accurately translated it as "visited"). When a shepherd visits a believer *where he or she lives*, the shepherd will often find a very different person than seen in a traditional, Sunday meeting. When shepherds go to the people *where they are*, they find out things about their lives. They get in, so to speak, to the real person's life, and they can then change things through the spiritual authority given them to do so. The need for various changes becomes obvious. The person acts like him or herself. Shepherds can then help the person apply the Word to their lives, and lasting changes can ensue.

Going to a person where he or she lives also gives a great deal of dignity to the person. Jesus did this with Zacchaeus and many others. Had he not gone to his house and had a personal encounter, Zacchaeus could not have been transformed so radically. Jesus said, "Salvation has come to this house" (Lk 19:9). That's what you bring when you go under Jesus' authority.

When you go, don't try to make anything happen. If there's a need, it will become known. You just go, be ready, and do whatever needs to be done. The Lord will open something up if it's in your parameters to deal with and if he wants it done at that time. It's an awesome thing when a shepherd cares for a sheep with authority from God. The phone and even e-mail these days can be used to "visit" God's People. However, I believe these can't substitute for physically going onto disciples' premises.

Note that for reasons of common sense and also for appearances sake, a shepherd should *always* be accompanied by at least one other person when going out to meet someone of the opposite sex.

How can such care be given for so many of God's People? Is such premium care really necessary for each of them? My answer is a big YES. Jesus bought them with his blood. Still, how can it be done time-wise? In a typical congregation there are many, many shepherds filling the seats who don't know they have this calling or that it exists. The Lord provides, in his Body, the gifts and callings needed to care for his Body. It's all there; now it must simply be recognized and utilized.

And by the way, you don't need permission from men to do your ministry. We must all be submissive to leadership, but our permission to minister comes from the Lord who called and gifted us and who will also judge us.

I know a brother who was called by the Lord as a shepherd and eventually identified as such by the Spirit through the Body of Christ. At that point he didn't know how to proceed. By God's grace, he didn't begin according to traditional assumptions. Somehow he had the humility to think to himself and ask the Lord, "What do I do now? Do I go out and get a building, advertise for meetings, etc.?" The Lord Jesus directed him to the verse I listed above in which God rebuked his shepherds for not visiting his sheep. Rather than building a regular meeting around himself or his ministry, something Jesus never did, he began visiting brothers and sisters. He oversaw and shepherded them. Through walking this out by the Spirit, he discovered the true shepherding ministry, which is a powerful provision for disciples. We need this ministry back.

I have discovered people considered "lay-men" with the calling and gifting of shepherd, doing various aspects of shepherding without knowing it. In one case, another friend of mine who was clearly a shepherd had a hard time conceiving he had this calling, since his life looked nothing like a "pastor." But he was clearly shepherding people. He didn't have a pulpit, but the truth is the shepherding ministry does not need a visible teaching platform.

I believe the answer for this friend and many, many others like him is to look outside the four walls of traditional-church structure and serve God's People by the Spirit. Just go for it, and know that as you're helping people you're fulfilling a much-needed role in the Body of Christ.

In conclusion, the office of shepherd must *radically* reform. Though shepherding may include arranging meetings—since these can provide care for sheep—their work is *not* characterized by being main speakers in the meetings of the Legislature. We will see later, especially in Chapter 33, that sharing in meetings is given to each member of the Legislature. The shepherding ministry does *not* primarily consist of building organizations either. It's to go to believers and build *them* up, make sure they're on the right track, etc. It's more like mentoring, though it may not be as in-depth as mentoring. This kind of care for people is invaluable, and it has been almost totally lacking in our traditional model and understanding.

Chapter 23
The Two Highest Ministries

A lot of emphasis has been put on the restoration of the "5-fold ministry" or "equipping-ministries" listed as gifts to the Body of Christ in Ephesians 4:11. This has been good because for hundreds of years the benefit of these was not accessed. However, we always need to keep in mind the two higher ministries than these five, given to every believer: *kings* and *priests*.

Satan is most afraid of these two ministries. And the development and operation of these by every believer is the goal of the five equipping-ministries.

A "king" in the Kingdom of God is obviously higher than a spokesperson for God (prophet) or a person sent by God as a master-carpenter (apostle), a shepherd, a reporter (evangelist), or a teacher. A king in the Kingdom of God includes being seated with Christ at the right hand of God. It's the highest place. And Christ was prophesied to be "a priest on his throne" (Zech 6:13). He is the King of kings and the High Priest we serve under. To be priests of God in this eternal, royal priesthood is a high, high calling.

The Temple in the Old Covenant illustrates what I'm saying for us. Before the Holy Place were five pillars. These represent the five equipping-ministries given to the Body by Jesus. Before the Holy of Holies were two pillars. These represent the ministries of every believer of king and priest.

Where the Roman traditional form of Christianity exists (among Catholics & Protestants), God's People are facing an identity crisis. The majority is somewhat debased; a minority is overly exalted. This began with the separation of clergy and laity/parishioners, and the elevation of the former over the latter. In this system, even if "parishioners" learn by revelation some of their identity in Christ, the traditional form and practice will downplay that reality, and most of them will lose it before long. In the Roman Catholic system, only some special believers are saints. Only some are priests. The moment a free, New Covenant believer mentally acknowledges a man over him as his priest, he loses his spiritual consciousness of his own priestly identity. The only elevated priest is the High Priest Jesus. We're all under him, on the same level.

The apostle Paul and the other apostles had such a high view of each faithful believer. They called them all saints. They wrote their epistles directly to them. The elders among them aren't even mentioned by name in the epistles. The People of God were so, so high in the estimation of the apostles, who worked to help them see this of themselves.

Phil 1:1 (NKJ): Paul and Timothy, bondservants of Jesus Christ, to all the *saints* in Christ Jesus who are in Philippi, with [or "including"] the [supervisors ("overseers")] and [food servers]...

Part of the Good News and a source of the believers' joy was the fact that they were all saints (holy, distinct, set apart ones)—what a high status!

One of the best things a true elder can do in his oversight and shepherding of holy ones is to keep himself on a level plane with them and push them forward to minister, watching over them as they do. When they try to lift him up, he can respond by lifting them up and reminding them of their high status and responsibility to minister. Actually, there's no higher plane than that of holy ones, but religious tradition has belittled and overlooked them.

It's in fallen human nature to want a human king more than God himself. There was a period when God, who himself redeemed Israel out of Egypt, was King of Israel. He enjoyed that role, and he defended his People through anointed judges.

But they just couldn't live by faith. They didn't want an invisible King. They rejected him for Saul. This has happened in the history of God's People over and over. The origin of hierarchical systems goes *way* back before the institution of the Roman Catholic Church and our other religious organizations. It's a human problem and a temptation for all of us. However, it must also be understood that our present form is *set up* according to this error.

I regularly attended a meeting of believers once in which the traditional pastor was very gifted. His messages were wonderful teaching and full of revelation from God. He was genuinely called and sent by God (though I think he was a teacher and prophet rather than an actual shepherd). Because of the Gospel he spoke and the fruit of the Spirit evidenced in his life, the whole group had a freedom and love from God. They loved strangers. They loved people from racial backgrounds other than their own. They served each other in love. There was a general trust among people too, very little suspicion. I witnessed all of this.

However, the pastor had a character flaw, as we all do, and it came out at one point. He did something clearly wrong. It was easily forgivable and not even that embarrassing, but it was wrong. So when a couple brothers found out about it, they confronted him, overcoming great fear to do so as they were under him in the human hierarchy. Unfortunately, although they were not accusative, he just couldn't humble himself and acknowledge that he had been wrong. He chose rather to leave, causing division and hurt as he left.

Had he not had an elevated status, he likely wouldn't have abused his authority as he wouldn't have had so much to abuse. He would've been protected from his own weaknesses which, again, we all have. If he had gotten out of line, the others could have confronted him easily and worked it out.

What happened next is an even greater tragedy. The group was very mature, I felt. People were led by the Spirit. People did outreach. Many there had been believers for many years. Several could publically teach. But because of tradition, which no one questioned, they felt they needed a man over them, a traditional pastor—in the line of Roman Catholic priests.

During the time when they had no pastor, they clung to the Lord. They kept their love for God. I was there once when the spiritual eyes of everyone in the room were opened to the Lord himself in a meeting, simultaneously. It was beautiful. But they thought they were missing something or that they were out of order without a man above them, a mediator between them and Jesus, I suppose. So they looked and looked and, finally, a man came.

When he did, he was like a wet blanket on a fire. They took him over the Lord as Head, just as the Israelites took Saul as king. His teaching was not life-giving, and gradually people lost the love and trust for each other they'd had. Some became legalistic. Joy left. It was a very sad scene. Many people didn't seem to notice the shift. I stuck around, prayed, and tried to help somehow, but eventually I had to leave. In my opinion, the group was at its height spiritually and ready to continue climbing during the time when they did not have a human as Head but were looking directly to the Lord.

Rather than follow tradition, a group can recognize Jesus' Headship among them and let everyone else take their place as, "members in particular" (1Cor 12:27). In fact, all members apart from the Head are in multiples; for example, there are two shoulders, two knees, two thumbs, two feet, etc. Jesus alone has a unique status in his Legislature. If a group does this, the people involved, including the elders, will receive revelation of the Lord. If they maintain this order, they'll receive more and more, be transformed into the same image, and walk in freedom (2Cor 3:18).

If you don't recognize your own authority, you will never act it out. So Satan's plan was to create a system that cloaks the reality of who believers are, so they don't use their authority to overcome and subdue him.

When Jesus walked this earth, he thrashed Satan and his kingdom really hard. Satan couldn't take it and eventually used all his strength to crucify Jesus. But really no one took Jesus' life; he laid it down willingly. That kind of love and obedience is outside Satan's ability to comprehend, expect, or believe. The devil fell right into the pit he dug. The Great Mystery (or "Secret") included the raising up of believers from all nations and seating them in Christ's Body, on his throne, while leaving them on Earth. From this highest of all places of authority, all believers can continue the thrashing Jesus began on Satan's kingdom, wherever they live! There are millions of believers now, all sharing in the authority of the risen Lord of Lords, all having Jesus the King in them, while on Earth. Now, "the manifold wisdom of God" is to "be made known through the Legislature to the rulers and the authorities in the heavenlies" (Eph 3:10).

This is happening, to a degree. However, tragically, the enemy is not taking the beating God intends—through every believer. One reason is that our current structure is keeping the majority of us from realizing and exercising our kingly authority and priestly ministries. With a few adjustments, we as the Body of Christ on Earth can and will become unstoppable. We will excel, far beyond what we can think or imagine, according to the power that will be allowed to work in and through us.

Chapter 24
The Healing of Three Breaches

There are three severe breaches that need to be healed in most of our Legislatures (citywide) today: between elders; between elders and the groups they serve; and between believers that are part of different regular meetings in the same city. We need to come together as brothers and sisters.

Elders located in the same city are always all in the same Legislature. Furthermore, elders of various cities are all in the same "One Body" of King Jesus. We all have the same goals: evangelizing, making disciples, and enduring to the end to stand approved before the Lord, who saved us, when he returns. Furthermore, within any group of believers, the overseers should not be lords over the people. They should not be like the current governmental systems of the world (Mt 20:25-28; Lk 22:25-27). They should not be a separate or higher class. They are brothers and sisters, fellow servants, fellow soldiers, fellow kings and priests, fellow believers with all of the distinct ones ("saints"), called out from the world into God's Legislature.

There's a small city in California where healing, miracles and outreach among believers has become the norm. A friend of mine who went there told me he could feel the presence of God tangibly upon entering that city. I heard one of the elders of that city say that once a week he and other leaders meet and "divide the spoil" of the victories each saw in his work. This kind of meeting for leaders who labor to give praise reports, pray for each other, etc. must be so glorious. These leaders have closed the gaps between each other. Still, I wonder if their meeting is open to all the elders in the Legislature of their city. If their unity is still based primarily on a particular organization, there's more to be done structurally.

To facilitate the spread outward and growth upward of the People of God, many new leaders will need to be appointed, regularly. And appointing elders is to "commend them to the Lord in whom they believed" (Ac 14:23). In other words, they are under the Lord and responsible to be led by the Spirit. They are not on a lower level than the servant who started the work or those who laid hands on and appointed them.

For a hierarchical top-leader to recognize people this way means giving up his recognition from believers of being one of a kind. It also means sharing funds with other leaders for their work (1Tim 5:17-18). It may be difficult, but this kind of humility causes people to fulfill their ministries. And recognizing them like this allows them to look up to the Lord himself, rather than a man above them, and in doing so the power of the Spirit will flow through them uniquely and uninhibitedly.

The challenge again goes back to our flawed way of thinking about the distribution of God's Legislatures. There is only one per city, and it needs many good leaders. Because we've taken on the opposite view—many ekklesia per city, each having *one* leader—we're very stifled in our ability to appoint new leaders needed for the work. We think to ordain new leaders means they each get a group for themselves, an expensive building to pay for, etc. In fact, it means they begin overseeing fellow believers in the city, spending time with them to make sure they're on track and fulfilling their ministries. There are to be many elders shepherding the one Flock in a city, and "*the* Chief Shepherd" is the only one above the others (see 1Pe 5:4).

On the same note, if no designation of "senior elder" is taken among the elders, it allows the Holy Spirit to utilize one elder more than others from time to time, according to what's best for everyone. This will also help the leaders keep from burning out. I heard one brother call this, "the wisdom of geese." He asked the Lord to help him understand leadership, and Jesus told him to study geese. He found that they often fly in a V formation with one leading the pack. When that one gets tired, it goes to the back and another bears the brunt of leadership for a while. This way they are not all slowed down by the first one's fatigue, and that one can also rest for a while. When leaders work together in this kind of a flexible leadership structure, each of their strengths will be utilized to meet various needs the Head wants to meet at various times.

The format of home-groups has become a great way to break larger, traditional groups into more personable ones. I just want to warn of one common scenario. Sometimes the leaders of home-groups are named as elders, but they are not allowed the room to exercise their authority fully. They are often placed under a man, the leader of an organization, who alone is considered having authority to serve the sheep. This seriously hampers their ministry and the development of sheep they can care for. I've seen good men severely hindered while trying to serve in this type of hierarchy. They don't have the confidence to stand up and serve with the power of God by the Holy Spirit.

One obstacle here may be related to who gets credit and glory before men. If one person is used to doing 90 or 95% of the ministering, it may be very hard for him to let loose 12 or 15 or 100 other leaders to minister *with full recognition of their ministries*. In other words, there will be pressure to keep them as part of a structural frame, under the first person.

Recognizing elders as having the same position among God's People will maintain freedom, under the Head, Jesus. He's the covering for the Legislature in the city, and all spiritual authority is derived from him.

You may wonder how order can be kept if there is no leader above the other leaders. It works by submission to one another, like the Bible teaches—including submission to those who aren't elders who also speak truth. Jesus can be your Head. When elders are gifted in various areas and to varying degrees, their gift will make room for them in the New Testament, Legislature. Where some are more advanced in various areas, those will be utilized by the Spirit as well. He knows what he's doing. Where true authority is given by the Lord, no fear need exist as to how to keep it. Leaders like this will want to see many other leaders responsibly raised up to work side by side with them, under Jesus—free.

As for the breach between the "clergy" and "parishioners/laypeople," I recommend leaders do whatever they can to heal it. A positive example of leaders getting free of the clergy-parishioner divide is found in Ted and Gayle Haggard's story. They were gracious enough to be interviewed at a meeting I attended, and the interview was allowed to be made public. So I feel at liberty to re-share some of their story.

The Haggards built a traditional-church of 14,000 attendees in Colorado of which they were the senior pastors. On a different level was likely a group of elders. (In much of Protestant Christianity there is a relationship between a person called "pastor" and a group called "elders" much like a Western corporation's CEO and board members). Ted was able to build this organization partly because of his genuine teaching gift. The group became so prominent that at one time he also sat as the head of an association of Evangelicals, which included 30 million members, and was in regular contact with the President of the US. He was about as high as you can get in this system. However, some fruit of this system was very disappointing.

Like everyone, Ted had wounds in his own heart. One of his was somewhat unique. I heard him share publicly, after his public fall and restoration, that he hadn't been healed of this by Jesus as he moved up in this system. As the organization he built grew, he said the challenges outside became greater than his internal development to be able to handle them. He was tempted according to an addictive cycle and would give in, in some limited ways. Afterward, he'd feel terrible and try hard to change himself again. This is common. Many of us have experienced the same cycle.

Ted's problem was eventually exposed publicly, and he and his wife, though repentant, were rejected. They were driven out of the church-organization they built and even out of the entire state of Colorado. I'm sure that not all the people in this organization rejected the Haggards, but the decision makers as a whole did. There was no help extended to them for restoration. It seems that many of the people in this system had lost the ability to show mercy, something each of us receives the moment we are given mercy to be born again.[18]

After Ted's "fall into grace," as he put it, he eventually got help from a Christian psychologist who knew how to help him, and he began to get genuine freedom with understanding.

We can learn many lessons from this, but let me point out one of them: too much separation between the Haggards, as senior pastors, and the rest of the believers in the group contributed to their problem. They could not be normal believers, possessing the ability to grow and learn from mistakes. When I heard the couple testify of their fall and restoration, Ted's wife, Gayle, made a wonderful statement. She said that though they had previously enjoyed a lot of success and prestige in their position, "Before, we were never the people. Now we are the people."[19]

It's important to the souls of leaders to be able to be on a level plane with the rest of the Body of Christ, while still being leaders. This will require choosing to be a servant *and* radical meeting reform.

When Communism attacked God's People severely in the USSR, they went back to some of the New Testament Scripture's practices. This helped everyone. In one case when a persecutor asked a Christian, *"Who is your leader?!"* in order to track him down, the person honestly answered, "We have no human leader."[20] There were elders in the underground Legislatures there, but believers also each learned of their connection to the One Head and their primary responsibility to be led by the Spirit themselves. They all saw him personally as their "One Leader" (Mt 23:10). We can make reforms back to

---

[18] Apparently many received this ability again. After the first edition of this writing, I got news that the ban on Ted and Gayle was lifted.
[19] Ted & Gayle Haggard, *Ted Haggard Uncensored* (Vancouver, WA: Living Hope Church, 2009), DVD.
[20] Richard Wurmbrand, *Tortured For Christ* (Bartlesville, OK: Living Sacrifice Book Company, 1967), 121. (Free copy currently available from torturedforchrist.com).

this kind of thinking without persecution hitting us first.

This change will also alleviate the burden currently on those in the traditional pastor role and on their wives. Jesus' yoke put on us is easy and his burden is light. No human can bear the position of Head or be responsible to take care of all the needs of believers. If someone attempts to take this role, he or she will get drained trying! It's a relief for a traditional pastor to step out of the role of Head and give it to the Lord, in the sight of God's People.

The third breach to heal is between believers in different groups in a city. In many cases, they've been told they belong to one group and that they are unstable or rebellious if they meet with other believers in their city. A generation ago this divide was much stronger. It has been weakening in some places because of more revealed truth and great changes in society. Just as physical cells need to be open to other healthy cells for nutrients to get through the whole body, every believer needs to be able to open his doors to every healthy believer in a city, and in the whole Body.

Believers *should* be encouraged to go here and there to receive, give, and be a part of various things. And they should know that they are securely in Jesus' Legislature in that city, under his Headship, regardless of which meetings they participate in.

Chapter 25
Re-centering Around Jesus Rather Than Individual Ministries

Jesus is the Foundation and the Head of his Legislature. He's even the one who builds it, as he said he would. We are co-laborers with God. When Paul and other apostles, master builders, laid the foundation of Jesus Christ for Legislatures, it's evident that they did not build them around their own personal ministries. Actually, looking at how they operated, these servants were somewhat out of the picture. They "engaged" the group to Jesus (2Cor 11:2); they set the foundation on him; they taught foundational truths; they prophesied; they cared for and watched over the Legislatures; they provided an example; they appointed elders to oversee the sheep; and they moved on. They continued to oversee the Legislatures—they prayed for them and continued to work with them—but it was often from the sidelines. They were not the focal point, nor was the local leadership.

The negative structural changes that began in the second century and were solidified by the Roman Government created groups of believers who were centered on a priest and his ministry to them. Another main focal point became the building they met in. I bring this up to make the connection between these historic actions and our current situation. In many Protestant church groups, I would say in the vast, vast majority of them, the group is focused almost exclusively on a brother's ministry rather than the Lord. By reforming our structure and meetings back to the pattern of the book of Acts, we will eliminate this problem and regain much more access to our Head. The good to come out of that will be so, so great—immeasurably great! ☺.

Teaching ministries are a very important aspect of Christianity, no doubt, but not all meetings should be centered on them. The New Testament meeting format can, at times include the exercise of everyone's ministry. At present, our groups are generally centered on one brother's ministry of teaching or exhortation. Apart from music ministry, generally other ministries functioning in our typical meetings are support ministries given to that brother, to support his weekly message. This is often a way God works with equipping ministries. They need certain support ministries, and so he links people together so that the Word goes forth. But there was much more to the original meetings of God's Legislatures than teaching—things we haven't been practicing.

We've seen earlier that cities/Legislatures are to eventually have elders appointed in them. A group that meets in a house or other building won't necessarily have elders in every meeting. However, when available, a good elder is extremely beneficial to believers, through his *oversight* (as long as he doesn't shift all focus to himself or take over most of the serving). Jesus spoke of meetings of believers in twos and threes in Matthew 18. He also assured them of his presence there. He didn't say this was conditional of having an elder present. The focus is on him. The meeting is to be around him.

Regardless of what ministries are present among us, we need to meet together and accomplish certain God-ordained objectives. And Jesus said the benefits of doing so are his presence, authority, and power, among other things.

I was part of a meeting of believers once for three years. In that time much growth in love, faith, and hope occurred. Much fruit came out of that very small group, both in the US and oversees. There was one interesting aspect of this meeting I'd like to share with you. Among the various believers with various functions, there was a brother there who was a shepherd. However, in three years of meetings with this group, I never once heard him give a teaching. There was teaching provided by others, and oversight provided by this shepherd. But the meetings we had were most often full participation meetings in which the focus was on the Lord.

Centering meetings on Jesus himself will result in freedom, spiritual exaltation and advancement, and many other wonderful things. Focusing meetings around individuals and their ministries will result in the benefits of that single ministry. Their ministries are great and necessary for the Body of Christ. However, I believe it's important to also provide meetings that are focused on the Lord and involve the exercise of many ministries, with full participation. I'll cover this in Chapter 33.

Consider again the following two pictures of leadership in the Old Testament. One is of Israel seeking and receiving a human king in place of God as their King. This came at great loss to Israel. The second was set up by God originally: the people all existed under and looked up to one King, God. He also gave them anointed judges who went throughout the land, led by the Spirit to defend Israel and ensure they were advancing safely toward their destiny. I believe this second picture is how leaders in the early Legislatures operated. We see a picture of it in the work of Peter, an overseer:

Acts 9:32-34 (NKJ): Now it came to pass, as Peter went through all parts of the country, that he also came down to the saints who dwelt in Lydda. There he found a certain man named Aeneas, who had been bedridden eight years and was paralyzed. And Peter said to him, "Aeneas, Jesus the Christ heals you. Arise and make your bed." Then he arose immediately.

Like Peter here, elders also moved about in their territories of responsibility and shepherded those who needed it. Jesus was the recognized King and Authority of the People, and overseers (apostles and elders) were like the judges of old. They moved about, watching out for God's People and tending to their needs.

It was always God's plan to give Israel a human king,

David, and to later sit his Son on David's throne. God is not threatened by human leadership, and he appoints it for his people (E.g., Moses). What he wants is for his People to recognize him as their King, first and foremost, and to honor and utilize the lower levels of leadership given for them as well. The positions of leadership among us are absolutely crucial for the development of God's People—no rebellion, suspicion, jealousy, or backbiting is ever allowed. These leaders speed up and make possible the advancement of the rest of the Sheep, because they've gone before us and made a way. They should ultimately help us see and obey our highest Leader better.

As far as we know, Peter and other true apostles and elders mentioned in the New Testament did not set up the kind of meetings we traditionally have. They served, yes, and room was made for them to teach. But they never set up "Legislatures" focused around themselves. As an example, Paul preached and taught from his house for two years in Rome (Ac 28:30-31). He did his ministry, but he didn't call those who benefitted the members of *his* Legislature—the Legislature in Rome was much bigger than that!

In other words, Paul was able to minister to people while allowing them to identify with a larger group and fulfill their ministries out in the world.

Our Legislatures need to be re-centered around Jesus. A sign we've done that will be that when believers meet for the first time they won't ask, "What church do you go to?" as much as, "Tell me about Jesus." People won't say, "I am of Paul; I am of Apollos; I am of Peter" (1Cor 1:12). They will lift up Jesus, and of course they will hold those who lead them in high esteem, those who exemplify endurance, growth and the fruit and power of the Spirit. But their view will be mainly on Jesus. ☺. People will gather in anticipation of meeting with him. The superstar mentality among us will be arrested. And Jesus will grow HUGE in our eyes.

Part 5: Original Christian Activities

Chapter 26
A Form That Holds The Spirit
(The Groundwork Laid Out in Acts)

The Legislature in Acts can be compared to a coral reef. It was full of variety, flexibility, and wonder. Jesus' earthly life and ministry was this way also. While he consistently did certain things—spent time with the Father, loved and served people, taught, evangelized, forced out demons, healed—the form in which he did these things was not always predictable. We see this flexibility continued on in his Body in Acts after he left. It is to be the way of his disciples today also, who he's given the same Spirit to:

John 3:8 (NKJ): The wind blows where it wishes, and you hear the sound of it, but cannot tell where it comes from and where it goes. So is everyone who is born of the Spirit."

The new birth is an introduction into a lifestyle that is unpredictable, life-giving, and powerful. Maturity means to be continually led by the Spirit (Rom 8:14).

Believers in Acts met in a variety of ways, for a variety of purposes. The character of leadership and the meetings organized were able to contain people born of and led by the Spirit. There was room to meet various needs and make quick changes successfully. This community was what Jesus was preparing to pour his Spirit into while he was on Earth. It was the new wineskin he trained his disciples to be.

Since the re-introduction of the Bible into modern languages (thank God), there have been several occasions of God pouring his Spirit out in a major way on his People. These have sometimes been called "revivals" or "outpourings." They amaze and affect hundreds, thousands, or millions of people. Unfortunately, though, in most cases they have not been sustained. The Spirit poured out was not retained. Often the People of God are left in a worse condition than before, facing greater challenges than previously. One of many tragic examples of this happened in North Korea.[21] Jesus said he was working to prevent this in the training of his disciples. He warned what would happen otherwise: "...the tear is made worse...the wineskins burst, the wine runs out, and the wineskins are ruined" (Mt 9:16-17).

We need to reform from centering on our traditional mass/service and having artificial boundaries to something flexible enough to hold all the aspects of Christianity. Our current form first began in the second and third centuries A.D. and was later influenced heavily by the Roman Empire. Leadership in it usually resembles that of non-regenerated groups of people (though today many good men and women often fill those positions and try their best in them). Since we each have access to the Spirit, the potential for explosive Christianity is in us. We need a leadership and meeting structure that continually fans the flames of people's hearts and helps them fulfill their ministries.

Most of the exciting activities of Christianity and the types of meetings of the early believers do not exist in our current practice. Just as a coral reef can't fit into a fish tank or even a swimming pool, these can't fit into our current form, so we have ignored and neglected them.

For a "tank" physically big enough to fit the variety of activities and meetings needed for the Legislature, we will need to shift our paradigm of the boundaries of an "ekklesia." As I taught extensively in Part 3 of this book, a "church" is not a

---

[21] P. Todd Nettleton, *North Korea: Good News Reaches the Hermit Kingdom* (Bartlesville, OK: Living Sacrifice Book Company, 2008).

physical structure, nor is it a meeting in a physical structure, nor an organization. It comprises all the believers and activities of believers in a city. We can no longer see a traditional meeting in a traditional place conducted by a traditional person as being more legitimate than two or three disciples meeting into Jesus' Authority (Mt 18:20).

Secondly, we will need to return to the original Legislatures' uses of many homes for meetings, as well as public places. Jesus first modeled this practice for us. His ministry included both meetings held in public, such as in synagogues or in nature, and in private, such as in the homes of Zacchaeus, Lazarus, and Simon's mother in law. His goal was not just quantity; it was quality. He needed to teach large crowds, yes, but he also needed to focus in on individuals. Going to a person's home brings great dignity to that person. It's unlikely that Jesus would've saved Zacchaeus without going to his house. So this is also one requirement of servants of the Word today in order to communicate God's love effectively and reach everyone God wants us to.

Meeting in people's homes can give access into people's hearts unlike meeting in public. It brings the Gospel and power of God into ordinary living situations. The strongholds in people's minds associated with designated religious buildings can be more easily bypassed in their homes, and great changes can result to their life.

In Acts, we see this practice continued by those Jesus had trained. First, among the Hebrew believers in Jesus:

Acts 2:46 (NKJ): So continuing daily with one accord in the temple, and breaking bread from house to house, they [ate together, praised God together, etc.]

Also among the Gentiles who believed later:

Acts 20:20-21 (NKJ): [Paul said:] I kept back nothing that was helpful, but proclaimed it to you, and taught you publicly and from house to house...

Related to this, let me point out that the Book of Romans reached the whole Legislature in Rome and multitudes of other people. Chapter 16 reveals how relational Paul was; he names 27 people by name in it. I believe his ability to be used to reach multitudes with this letter came partly through his devotion to individual relationships. Meeting in homes can facilitate that.

Although public places are not sanctuaries according to Scripture (see Ac 17:24; 1Cor 6:19; Heb 9:24, 10:19-22), they are very useful, when possible, for large-scale meetings. This should never be forgotten. The verse above speaks of both, larger public meetings and meetings in homes. To only meet in homes is only half of the picture laid out for us in Acts.

Acts 5:42 (NASB): Daily in the temple, and from house to house, they kept right on teaching and preaching Jesus as the Christ.

Our great evangelistic meetings today, that bring thousands to faith, often result in a small increase in traditional-church attendance. Thousands came to the Lord in Acts too, but they were immediately plugged into a system, community and lifestyle conducive to their growth and eventual full expression.

At the end of the first complete public proclamation of the Good News after Jesus ascended, the following took place:

Acts 2:37-41 (NKJ): Now when they heard this, they were cut to the heart, and said to Peter and the rest of the apostles, "Men and brethren, what shall we do?" Then Peter said to them, "Repent, and let every one of you be [immersed] in the name of Jesus Christ for the remission of sins; and you shall receive the gift of the Holy Spirit. For the promise is to you and to your children, and to all who are afar off, as many as the Lord our God will call." And with many other words he testified and exhorted them, saying, "Be saved from this perverse generation." Then those who gladly received his word were [immersed]; and that day about three thousand souls were added to them.

These 3000 souls needed to be cared for. They needed an environment to grow up in. God's children should be given the best environment to grow in. The one provided by the apostles and elders for the earliest believers included five main activities. They are described immediately after the passage above:

Acts 2:42-47 (NASB): They were continually devoting themselves to the apostles' teaching and to fellowship, to the breaking of bread and to prayer. [Fear was coming upon every soul]; and many wonders and signs were taking place through the apostles. And all those who had believed were together and had all things in common; and they began selling their property and possessions and were sharing them with all, as anyone might have need. Day by day continuing with one mind in the temple, and breaking bread from house to house, they were taking their meals together with gladness and sincerity of heart, praising God and having favor with all the people. And the Lord was adding to their number day by day those who were being saved.

So, we see that the first disciples benefitted from the following provisions or activities:

1. Teaching
2. Fellowship and eating together (incl. the Lord's Supper)
3. Financially caring for each other
4. Prayer, praise, and other priestly work
5. Evangelism

Before delving into these activities, I should say that the foundation for them from the beginning was being born again through believing the Gospel and bowing to Jesus as Lord, also immersion in water as a pledge toward discipleship and immersion in the Holy Spirit for power to be a witness.

The Lord died for us, and he immerses with the Holy Spirit and fire (Mt 3:11; Mk 1:8; Lk 3:16; Jn 1:33; Ac 1:5, 11:16). He commanded his disciples to do nothing concerning the Great

Commission until the Holy Spirit had fallen on them (Ac 1:4). Throughout the book of Acts, when new believers were added to the Legislature after the day of Pentecost, they were also immersed in the Holy Spirit by the Lord. Sometimes this was done through the laying on of hands, sometimes it wasn't, but leaders and others worked to make sure disciples received it from the Lord (see Ac 8:14-17, 9:17, 19:1-7, 2:38-39).

Having been subjected to the Dark Ages, the Legislature lost the knowledge of most Scriptural truth. This included the new birth, the righteousness which is by faith, immersion in water, and many others, including immersion in the Holy Spirit and the gifts of the Spirit. However, the Word of God never changed. Restoring each precious Biblical truth has been a fight. Satan's surrounded each one with controversy, confusion, and division. Rediscovering each one is like finding a diamond or precious stone in the earth. It's required a lot of digging, but to recover each one is worth all the work.

Rediscovering the original Christian activities, along with the many other things we've looked at in this book already, will propel us forward spiritually and make room for more of God's will to be done among us and through us on Earth.

Chapter 27
Activity #1: Teaching

Acts 2:42 (NASB): And they were continually devoting themselves to the apostles' teaching...

This is the first practice recorded of this newly born Legislature. It's also one of its main functions as "the Legislature, the pillar and support of the truth" (1Tim 3:15). Good teaching is vital to Christianity. Where the Gospel is taught well, the effect is very evident. Without it, God's People don't have fuel to do other Christianity activities very well.

Faith comes from hearing God speak, which happens through his Word and good teaching, among other ways (Rom 10:17, 1Tim 4:6, Gal 3:2, 5). The benefits of this faith are so many:

1. Good works can be added to faith (Rom 1:5, 1Thes 1:3, Jas 2:22, 2Pe 1:5)
2. Faith is how believers are established and strengthened (Col 2:7)
3. Faith is the basis we resist Satan on (1Pe 5:9). It makes up half of our breastplate, which protects the heart (1Thes 5:8)
4. It's the basis of God's edification of believers (1Tim 1:4)
5. Holding to faith is one way hope increases (Rom 15:13)
6. Faith is how prayers are answered (Mark 11:24; Jas 1:6, 5:15)
7. It's exceedingly precious, more so than any trial we will go through (1Pe 1:7)
8. Without faith, it's impossible to please God (Heb 11:6)

Believers sometimes struggle in our lives, trying to do what we know in our minds is right. Often one of our problems is that we are not filled with enough truth:

Col 3:16 (NKJ): Let the word of Christ dwell in you richly in all wisdom, teaching and admonishing [i.e., "cautioning or gently reproving"] one another...

When we're full of the word of Christ, heavenly realities are before our eyes. Deception has a much harder time affecting us.

2 Pet 1:4 (NKJ): ...through [exceedingly great and precious promises] you may be partakers of the divine nature, having escaped the corruption that is in the world through lust.

The promises and all other aspects of God's truth need to be continually taught and proclaimed for and by God's People so that we can all see clearly and trade off the things of the world for the Kingdom.

Notice that Colossians 3:16 (above) instructs all disciples to let the Word dwell in them richly *and* to use it, with wisdom, to teach others.

Eph 4:15 (NKJ): ...speaking the truth in love, [we] may grow up in all things into Him who is the head—Christ.

This activity is for each believer, though some will teach more often, to more people, or in a more foundational capacity—providing truth disciples will use to teach each other with.

Considering Acts 2:42 again, it's very important to note that the new believers were devoting themselves to the "apostle*s'* teaching" (plural). There were multiple people teaching the Gospel to believers at the same time. And their teaching was with the vision that those who were taught would teach others afterward:

2 Tim 2:2 (NKJ): And the things that you have heard from me among many witnesses, commit these to faithful men who will be able to teach others also. (see also Mt 28:20).

Through structural reform, people who are taught can be given opportunity to teach others. In this way, teaching will be continually done on various levels.

There are many aspects of the Gospel. They need to be taught to different people, at different times, and by different people. It is very important for believers to receive a "balanced diet" of teaching. Just as a complete meal contains various types of vegetables, bread, meat, etc., believers need to receive teaching from several people. If a person eats only beans all his life, he will be nutritionally deficient. Just adding rice to beans creates a whole new, complete protein. Growing believers need to be exposed to a variety of teaching from a variety of people.

In addition to teaching, we should also have times set aside for public Scripture reading, in which we just hear and submit to the Scripture, without much or any human commentary (1Tim 4:13, 1Thes 5:27, Col 4:16-17, Lk 4:16-17).

Consider also the following verse.

Heb 5:12 (NKJ): For though by this time you ought to be teachers, you need someone to teach you again the first principles of the oracles of God; and you have come to need milk and not solid food.

Many of those who are currently being taught also need to be teaching. More teaching opportunities will benefit those who will be taught and those who will teach.

One thing that may stand in our way from this is fear in leadership of not being able to oversee and quality-control all the teaching. For sure, there must be caution and accountability for those who are teaching. However, with thousands upon thousands of new believers to teach, eventually there was no time for the first apostles or elders to be present and hear all the teaching going on. There isn't enough time to physically check out all the teaching God desires to be going on today either.

Instead, what will help with this are some basic foundational truths, such as:

1. Teachers are accountable to the Lord for what they teach and will be judged by him strictly on it; they should be conscious of this (Jas 3:1)
2. Teachers and others who teach need to submit to elders and apostles who have responsibility for the souls of sheep. Especially in the case of those less "tried and true," it's very important they be given oversight and stay submissive to it (1Tim 1:3-4, 1Pe 5:5)
3. We all have in us an abiding anointing from God, the Spirit of Truth, who will teach them. We're to test everything by him (1Jn 2:20-21, 4:1; Jn 6:45; Heb 8:11; 2Pe 3:17)
4. The Bible, the Word of God, is perfect and useful to test with (Ps 19:7, 2Tim 3:16, Jn 10:35)
5. No one will teach perfectly, but truth is primarily the Lord, not a doctrine, so expect and tolerate mistakes (Jn 14:6)
6. Every disciple is responsible to not tolerate those who teach seriously false doctrines (Rev 2:20, 1Tim 6:20, Phil 3:2)
7. We're also to beware of those who teach truth hypocritically (Lk 20:46). We're not to invite them into our houses or greet them (2Jn 10-11). We're to turn away from them (2Tim 3:5).

It will actually be healthy for believers to be empowered with these truths and allowed to exercise their ability to test teaching by the Spirit and the Scriptures. They will grow by doing so. Rather than being present to approve or disapprove every teaching *for* disciples, elders do better by teaching them to test and letting them do so for themselves. This will allow them to become "the mature, who because of practice have their senses trained to discern good from evil," enabled to eat "solid food" (Heb 5:14). If believers are temporarily mistaken or deceived, which happens very often, they will be strengthened as they're helped out of it through ongoing oversight.

Eventually, we need to be able to say what Paul said to the Legislature in Rome:

Rom 15:14 (NKJ): Now I myself am confident concerning you, my brethren, that you also are full of goodness, filled with all knowledge, able also to admonish one another.

Chapter 28
Activity #2: Fellowship

Acts 2:42 (NASB): They were continually devoting themselves to the apostles' teaching *and to fellowship*, to the *breaking of bread...*

Acts 2:46 (NASB): *breaking bread* from house to house, they were taking their meals together with gladness and *sincerity* of heart...

Jesus' oversight of his disciples while here on earth included making sure they loved each other:

John 15:12-14, 17 (NKJ): This is My commandment, that you love one another as I have loved you. Greater love has no one than this, than to lay down one's life for his friends. You are My friends if you do whatever I command you...These things I command you, that you love one another.

The early disciples continued to teach and oversee the growth of love after Jesus left, making sure it happened. The following are some of the many statements in the New Testament which show that Paul was concerned with the faith *and* the love (not to mention the hope) of God's People he oversaw.

Eph 1:15-16 (NKJ): Therefore I also, after I heard of *your faith* in the Lord Jesus *and your love* for all the saints, do not cease to give thanks for you, making mention of you in my prayers...

Col 1:3-4 (NKJ): We give thanks to the God and Father of our Lord Jesus Christ, praying always for you, since we heard of *your faith* in Christ Jesus *and of your love* for all the saints...

1 Thes 3:6-7 (NKJ): But now that Timothy has come to us from you, and brought us good news of *your faith and love*, and that you always have good remembrance of us, greatly desiring to see us, as we also to see you—therefore, brethren, in all our affliction and distress we were comforted...

2 Thes 1:3 (NKJ): We are bound to thank God always for you, brethren, as it is fitting, because *your faith* grows exceedingly, *and the love* of every one of you all abounds toward each other...

Faith comes from hearing God's Words. However, as James taught, to have faith without resulting works is worthless. Faith must be expressed through love and works.

Gal 5:6 (NASB): For in Christ Jesus neither circumcision nor uncircumcision means anything, but faith working through love.

The goal of New Covenant teaching is *love*:

1 Tim 1:5 (NKJ): Now the purpose of [our instruction] is *love*...

1 Cor 13:13 (NKJ): And now [out of this fleeting moment that we have at this time, what will] abide [are] faith, hope, love, these three; but the greatest of these is love.

Through the provision of teaching, faith comes to those who hear God's Words. Hope also becomes available through that faith received. However, for the full package of faith, hope, *and love,* the provision of fellowship is given, among others. Any collection of Christian activities offered God's People that does not produce faith, hope, *and* love in them is incomplete. It won't stand the test of fire on the Great Day (1Cor 3:12-13).

Jesus washed his disciples' feet before commanding them to love each other as he loved them. This was a demonstration of how to love people. It's through serving each other:

Gal 5:13 (NKJ): ...through love serve one another.

This love is practical and relational. It grows in a community of believers who get to know and trust each other:

1 Cor 13:4-7 (NIV): Love is patient, love is kind. It does not envy, it does not boast, it is not proud. It is not rude, it is not self-seeking, it is not easily angered, it keeps no record of wrongs. Love does not delight in evil but rejoices with the truth. It always protects, always trusts, always hopes, always perseveres.

Peter describes how love is to work among us:

1 Pet 1:22-23 (NKJ): Since you have purified your souls in obeying the truth through the Spirit in sincere love of the brethren, love one another fervently with a pure heart, having been born again...

We see here that the basis of our ability and responsibility to love one another is the new birth. Our new nature is one of love. However, once we have been given that love, there is a process of purification that must take place in our souls. This takes place *in action* by growing together, supporting each other, etc. Shortly after this verse Peter reveals the aspect of God's People as his Temple:

1 Pet 2:5 (NKJ): …as living stones, [you] are being built up [into] a spiritual house…

In God's Temple, each of us is a living stone. We are being fitted next to each other as God builds us into a spiritual house. This process takes place as we get to know one another. However, there is pain involved in this. We have to make adjustments to get along and serve God together. In doing so, though, we learn to appreciate one another, utilize one another's strengths, and support one another. This process is one of the opportunities given us by God during this age—the time between Jesus' first and second coming. To miss this, no matter how much teaching we may get, we remain undeveloped, rugged stones, not fitted into the rest of the Temple, undeveloped in character.

Teaching, or any other kind of ministering in a public meeting, does not require much change of character. There's not much of a need to fit together as living stones in this format. A person can minister publically for many years, his gift operating as he does, and his character can remain undeveloped in many ways. Why? He wasn't subjected to the friction of being fitted together with other living stones.

Many commands found in the New Testament simply cannot be obeyed in a teaching-meeting format. Teaching requires little or no interaction with people. The time before and after a teaching on a Sunday morning is not long enough to get to know one another either. Here are just some of these commands that require more than teaching meetings to be carried out:

- "Be devoted to one another in brotherly love, in honor giving preference to one another" (Rom 12:10)
- "Love one another" (this exact phrase occurs 15 times in the NT) (Rom 13:8)
- "Accept one another" (Rom 15:7)
- "Instruct one another" (Rom 15:14)
- "Be perfectly joined together in the same mind and judgment" (1Cor 1:10)

- "Bear one another's burdens and so fulfill the law of Christ" (Gal 6:2)
- "…be filled with the Spirit, speaking to one another" (Eph 5:19)
- "Submit to one another out of fear of Christ" (Eph 5:21)
- "Bear with each other and forgive whatever grievances you may have against one another" (Col 3:13)
- "Comfort and edify one another" (1Thes 5:11)
- "Encourage one another daily" (Heb 3:13)
- "Confess your sins to one another and pray for one another that you may be healed" (Jas 5:16)
- "Be hospitable to one another without grumbling" (1Pe 4:9)
- "Have fellowship with one another" (1Jn 1:7)

The Greek word for fellowship, "koinonia," could have been translated "participation," "sharing," or "communion." This "koinonia," or "fellowship," is a special privilege given only to those who fulfill two specific requirements: being in a relationship with God through the New Covenant, and walking honestly in the light.

Considering the first requirement, a covenant brings people together. Through it, we lay down our lives and thereby gain a new life which is committed to the other party to the death. Those who enter a covenant gain the privilege of special union and relationship with the other parties involved. The Biblical covenants are almost always made through the shedding of the blood of a sacrifice. In our case, it was the blood of Jesus:

Mark 14:23-24 (NKJ): Then He took the cup, and when He had given thanks He gave it to them, and they all drank from it. And He said to them, "This is My blood of the new covenant, which is shed for many."

All drank, and as they drank, they entered the covenant together. So they were now all related vertically to Jesus and the Father and horizontally to each other. When we believed the Gospel and bowed to the Lord Jesus, we entered the covenant. The blood of Jesus was applied to our lives. Once we're in, we have the right to fellowship with each other and to take communion together, the Lord's Dinner. Paul set this kind of meal in place in the Legislatures he established:

1 Cor 11:23-26 (NKJ): For I received from the Lord that which I also delivered to you: that the Lord Jesus on the same night in which He was betrayed took bread; and when He had given thanks, He broke it and said, "Take, eat; this is My body which is broken for you; do this in remembrance of Me." In the same manner He also took the cup after supper, saying, "This cup is the new covenant in My blood. This do, as often as you drink it, in remembrance of Me." For as often as you eat this bread and drink this cup, you proclaim the Lord's death till He comes.

Notice verse 26. As often as we do this, we're making a spiritual proclamation of Jesus' death as we look ahead to his return. It's extremely powerful. We're remembering him and that we're in a covenant with him and each other. Knowing this, we should continually practice it.

Paul said to the Legislature in Corinth:

1 Cor 11:20-21 (NKJ): Therefore when you come together in one place, it is not to eat the Lord's Supper. For in eating, each one takes his own supper ahead of others; and one is hungry and another is drunk.

Notice here that their Lord's Supper ceremony, as Paul taught them, was an actual meal. I suggest we reform back to the New Testament model of taking the Bread and Wine (or Juice) along with eating a full meal together. That's the way it was originally done, and I think it was to enjoy the fellowship that results from the covenant.

Scripture is very flexible about how to eat the Lord's Supper. It is a ceremony, but it's simple; there's no set format for it. It can be done as frequently as you'd like, with as many or as few people as you'd like. We're instructed to give thanks, bless the cup, and break the bread (1Cor 11:24, 10:16). We're to be aware that we are doing it in remembrance of him and proclaiming his death powerfully. We're to expect blessing as it is a powerful reiteration of our covenant, and we're to fear judgment for taking it wrongly (1Cor 10:16, 11:26-27). As the verse above shows, we need to be concerned with each other in the process. We are to have fellowship with each other in it, acknowledging our covenant with each other. Along these lines, there is a large variety of activities that can accompany this meal. People can pray and share before the whole group or at each individual table or both. The Spirit will lead as we launch out in obeying the Word, and we will learn a lot in the process.

There have been reports of major healing and miracles taking place through taking communion together with love, faith, and expectation. The benefits of the covenant, made with the sacrifice of Jesus' body, are way beyond our ability to count. The riches are unsearchable. This ceremony is one way God has given us in order to access them. I myself have been healed and received freedom powerfully through this provision several times. Once it's implemented among believers regularly, along with their other spiritual needs being provided for, it will be a powerful means that the Lord can bless his people through. This was his intention in giving it to us, though the vast majority of us are somewhat neglecting it at this time.

Now let's consider the second requirement for fellowship, that believers be walking in the light—honestly walking according to the truth of the Gospel:

I Jn 1:7 (NKJ): But if we walk in the light as He is in the light, we have fellowship with one another, and the blood of Jesus Christ His Son cleanses us from all sin.

I believe the order in Acts 2 is significant. First, it mentions teaching; then, it mentions fellowship. Also, in Ephesians 4, the provision of equipping-ministries is mentioned first, then the Body building itself up. Believers need good teaching and help from these gifts to the Body in order to have something to share with each other. Without the true Good News being taught, people cannot walk in the light well, and this would negatively affect fellowship.

Having fellowship with one another includes partnering together, communicating, exchanging, sharing faith with each other through words we speak to each other. It takes time and energy, so a format is required to facilitate it. Few believers will get together and do this on their own. It's up to leadership, especially apostles and elders, to make sure this is part of the lifestyle of believers they oversee. Disciples without good oversight, who learn this responsibility, must make their own effort to likewise "continually devote themselves to fellowship."

Acts 2 states that they had *fellowship* and *the breaking of bread*, from *house to house*, with *sincerity*. Eating together in homes helps facilitate fellowship. They "continually devoted themselves...to the breaking of bread." Larger meetings, held in larger buildings, can also include fellowship. A large meeting with food was described in Acts 6. Another was described in 1Corinthians 11, which we've looked at. In other places, an established meeting called a "love feast" was used to facilitate fellowship among large groups (see 2Pe 2:13, Jude vs. 12). It's a major part of *why* they met:

Acts 20:7 (NASB): On the first day of the week, when we were gathered together to break bread...

This breaking bread together that they "continually devoted themselves to" is a vital part of New Testament Christianity. Let's bring it back.

Acts 2:46 says they met with *sincerity*. Our fellowship meetings must be kept sincere. This is one of the litmus tests leaders should use in their oversight. If honest sincerity is lost, a person or group has gone into darkness and hypocrisy. This was the main problem Jesus had with religious leaders in his day, and it contributed to their rejection of him, the Truth. When that happens, leaders need to help people find their way back to walking in the light. Insincerity is a sign people are off the foundation of righteousness and acceptance by Jesus' blood. It's *crucial* we maintain sincerity. Part of the power of the Gospel is that it makes us increasingly sincere, and we don't want to lose progress in that:

1 Tim 1:5 (NKJ): Now the purpose of [our instruction] is love *from a pure heart*, from a *good conscience*, and from *sincere faith*.

2 Tim 3:1-2,5 (NKJ): ...in the last days [some evil people will be] having a form of godliness but denying its power. And from such people turn away!

1 Cor 5:11 (NASB): But actually, I wrote to you not to associate with any so-called brother if he is an immoral person, or covetous, or an idolater, or a reviler, or a drunkard, or a swindler—not even to eat with such a [person].

2 Thes 3:14-15 (NKJ): And if anyone does not obey our word in this epistle, note that person and do not keep company with him, that he may be ashamed. Yet do not count him as an enemy, but admonish ["caution or gently reprove"] him as a brother.

3 John 1:3-4 (NASB): For I was very glad when brethren came and testified to your truth, how you are walking in truth. I have no greater joy than this, to hear of my children walking in the truth.

Notice from this last verse that the apostle John's *greatest* joy wasn't packed out conferences or mass evangelism, miracles, healings, deliverances from jails (as recorded in Acts)—those would surely follow—but his greatest joy was to see believers he'd raised walking in sincerity, in the truth.

In meetings or times within meetings devoted to fellowship, everyone must be able to share truth with each other. No one person should take over the meeting and turn it into a teaching meeting. Each brother and sister is equal and must equally be allowed to share what's on their heart.

In this kind of a meeting, everyone is to be mindful of the Head and led by the Spirit. 1Corinthians 2:16 says, "*We* have the mind of Christ." I've seen that in order to be in sync with the Head in a meeting like this, we may need to find his mind collectively. No human is to take the place of the Head in these meetings. No one is to be allowed to. To get the benefit of the Head in these meetings, we will have to tolerate and listen to each other to discover his will *together* and go with it.

If you start meeting this way, some people in the group will face the temptation to assume leadership of the meetings. If you can get past this, you'll get to the good stuff. To have Jesus involved as Head, people have to really take a backseat, especially older, more experienced people.

Another temptation will be to try to make the meeting fit a certain image or form, especially for those who've gotten used to meetings like that. Most of us have our mental ideas of what religious meetings are to be like, but to let the Spirit lead we'll have to dismiss those ideas. When our first priority is giving the Head free reign, we'll proceed somewhat cautiously and he'll lead. I heard it said recently, "When you're in control, Someone else isn't!"

There's a fear of failure we have to put to death. We see it in an example in the Old Testament. The Ark of the Covenant had been taken from Israel, and through God's help King David was able to recover it. While they were transporting it back, the oxen pulling the cart must have stumbled because it was about to fall. One of the men leading the cart, Uzzah, must have thought, "I need to help God here," and grabbed it to keep it up. As a result, "the anger of the LORD burned against Uzzah, and God struck him down there for his irreverence" (2 Samuel 6:7). We have to resist the temptation to try to "help" God by taking control when it looks to us like He's going to fail in a meeting. He won't fail.

Regarding full participation, Jesus is in each of us, and to get the full benefit of Christianity we will need to experience God's grace through each person using his or her gift:

1 Pet 4:10-11 (NKJ): As each one has received a gift,

minister it to one another, as good stewards of the manifold grace of God. If anyone speaks, let him speak as the oracles of God. If anyone ministers, let him do it as with the ability which God supplies, that in all things God may be glorified through Jesus Christ, to whom belong the glory and the dominion...

A format must be provided through which the streams from the river of God flow out of people to make the city of God glad, "to profit everyone":

Ps 46:4 (NKJ): There is a river whose streams shall make glad the city of God, the holy place of the tabernacle of the Most High.

1 Cor 12:7 (NKJ): The [presentation] of the Spirit is given to each one for the profit of all [or, "to bring all together"].

There are some needs in our lives, including physical healing, freedom from evil spirits, wisdom, knowledge, etc., that, at times, *cannot* be fulfilled without everyone ministering. I believe one reason some aren't healed though prayed for by great men and women of God is that the healing for their case is in a more "ordinary" believer, maybe one they hadn't considered or wouldn't normally go to. It's dormant in that person because we've lacked a format that facilitates the Body serving *each other*. God provides for us through individuals who are gifts to the Body and through *each* member of the Body serving each other. He also provides through the Head directly. By not utilizing all of these, we miss out on some of the healing, miracles, encouragement, and other good things he has for us.

One of the greatest tragedies is that believers have the Anointed One in them and, therefore, massive amounts of power in them, but through tradition and our meeting formats, they never get to use it. This is truly one of the reasons God's People are not "glad." We're missing out on the River of God in each of us.

In a meeting for fellowship, all believers speak.[22] No one just listens. In this setting, the actual growth of the Body of Christ occurs as each member does its part:

Eph 4:15-16 (NKJ): ...speaking the truth in love, [we] may grow up in all things into Him who is the head—Christ—from whom the whole body, joined and knit together by what every joint supplies, according to the effective working by which every part does its share, causes growth of the body for the edifying of itself in love.

Of course this cannot be done in a teaching meeting format and it will require a good amount of time. In this setting, believers' souls are cared for as they are able to express themselves to others in a personal way. Connections are made. The Lord puts different people together. Relationships are formed. Questions are answered. Testimonies are celebrated. We can "weep with those who weep and rejoice with those who rejoice" (Rom 12:15). Burdens are carried. We heal each other's wounds from battle through this kind of meeting, as we speak truth by the Spirit and deal with real issues together. People are able to share what God is doing in their lives and families. Each person gives and receives.

This kind of care for the soul is what the world and so many of God's People are longing for. It's necessary for a healthy life.

We need this aspect of Christianity restored so that we can make it to the finish line of enduring to the end. Even Jesus needed God to provide Simon of Cyrene to help him carry his cross. We can't win totally alone. Christianity is to be lived out as a Body. Once, during a fellowship meeting I was in, the Lord revealed to one of us that how strong we are is not measured by our personal strength, but by how strong our relationships are.

Without help from others, there are some things we can be

---

[22] Not *necessarily* public speaking or sharing before the whole group, though that's also possible and profitable; people can share, teach, encourage, and inquire of each other one on one or in small groups, while eating, e.g.

overpowered by, some burdens we can't bear alone at times:

Eccl 4:9-12 (NKJ): Two are better than one, because they have a good reward for their labor. For if they fall, one will lift up his companion. But woe to him who is alone when he falls, for he has no one to help him up. Again, if two lie down together, they will keep warm; but how can one be warm alone? Though one may be overpowered by another, two can withstand him. And a threefold cord is not quickly broken.

Addictions are tormenting. Sometimes addictions are instantly driven away from people by the power of the Holy Spirit. In other cases they are allowed by God to remain. He requires a person to wrestle with the spirit behind it and gain victory over time. This is revealed clearly in Scripture and experience, and there's an important reason God works this way (Judges 3:1-2). But regardless of how it comes, God promises victory over them all for us. ☺. And part of the provision he gives is regular fellowship. The transparency required brings issues into the open to be dealt with.

In a teaching setting, transparency is not required. But believers need transparency to help them make hard, life-changing decisions. Fellowship provides godly peer pressure, essential at times for success in Christianity. Regular fellowship in a small group setting forces transparency. A person is encouraged to put the things learned from teaching into practice in his or her private life this way. The person will either choose to do so or to leave, but not to stay and continue with ups and downs indefinitely. In this environment, people can "let [their] progress be evident to all" (1Tim 4:15).

Had the Legislature not lost the activity of sincere fellowship, there would have been no need for Alcoholics Anonymous. It was started by a Christian in order to meet the gaping need of so many. It also encountered great resistance from traditional church-organization leadership. If we are going to bring to Christ drug addicts, abusers, prostitutes, pimps, pornographers, murderers, fornicators, etc., as God wants us to, we are going to need to offer them this care for their souls. In actuality, it's needed by every human being God has created and who's been born again. It complements the power of evangelism, regular teaching, prophecy and shepherding.

Good relationships give us strength to hold an inflow of new believers, as each relationship is like a cord on a net. Also, our trust for one another will allow us to pray together more powerfully and do outreach together powerfully. And the world will recognize we are Jesus' disciples by our love for each other (Jn 13:35). So our evangelism will also become more effective through our fellowship.

In a meeting or time devoted to fellowship, God is able to be glorified through the conversation of *every* believer. (In a large group context, people talk with those at their table or circle). In such a case many people speak simultaneously, so God is glorified with many words in a short time. And God *loves* it. As recorded in Malachi:

Mal 3:16-17 (NKJ): Then those who feared the LORD *spoke to one another*, and the LORD listened and heard them; so a book of remembrance was written before Him for those who fear the LORD and who meditate on His name. "They shall be Mine," says the LORD of hosts, "On the day that I make them My jewels. And I will spare them as a man spares his own son who serves him."

This kind of interaction existed in the gatherings referred to in Hebrews:

Heb 10:24-25 (NASB): Let us consider how to stimulate one another to love and good deeds, not forsaking our own assembling together, as is the habit of some, but *encouraging one another;* and all the more as you see the day drawing near.

Fellowship needs to be viewed as being *as important* as teaching. If people are not willing to learn to love, they should not be entrusted with truth. This is brought out in Scripture:

Col 2:2 (NIV): My purpose is that they may be encouraged in heart and united in love, so that they may have the full riches of complete understanding, in order that they may know...

Without a devotion to love, God will not reveal much truth to us. The activity of fellowship is one main way we grow in love for one another, so it will enhance teaching and allow for more revelation. It will also cause the teaching received to be solidified in those who hear, as they will turn around and "teach one another" (Rom 15:14, Col 3:16).

There is a problem commonly occurring today in the Body of Christ. Believers are hearing good teaching in meetings, but then it's leaking out of their lives during the time in between meetings. The result is that they don't get the intended benefit from the Word they heard. Even worse, they experience more judgment in their lives, being accountable to more truth. They can also get proud through so much knowledge, making them less reachable later. "Knowledge puffs up, but love builds up" (1Cor 8:1). The fellowship aspect of Christianity is part of the remedy for this.

We're called in Scripture, "God's Family" (Eph 3:14-15, 1Pe 4:17). We're not to be *only* like a classroom. We're also to be like a family because we're all brothers and sisters under God the Father. Among those Timothy was serving, Paul instructed him to relate to, "an older man...as a father, the younger men as brothers, the older women as mothers, and the younger women as sisters" (1Tim 5:1-2). God wants his People to be in relationship with each other. He's not content with us remaining strangers.

One of the major reasons believers backslide so often among us is that they are not fulfilled relationally. They go to meetings, sometimes for many hours per week, but they never get to really know anyone. This can go on for years (by the way, a test of how well you know people is how much you trust them and vice versa—for example with money or children). Life, socially, was more exciting and fulfilling for many of us before we were born again. In the current system, we're often left with an empty place inside we are trying to fill. It's to be filled with the missing aspect of fellowship, which God's Legislatures had at first.

In chapter 8, I recorded a dream a friend of mine had regarding reformation. Later, on November 1, 2009 this same friend had another dream, regarding a future fellowship meeting:

> Thirty or forty family and friends had gathered for some kind of a get together. It was not a meeting for 'church' as we normally think of it. There was a strong but different presence of God among us. We were being changed in amazing ways. Our lives carried a different feel or aura. It resembled Christianity as we had known it but was far advanced. We were still on earth dealing with life and circumstances, but in a whole new spirit. Those who had been through the 'fire' seemed to be more schooled by the Spirit in prayer and faith. When they spoke or prayed, it was in cooperation with the Lord and things happened. People and circumstances changed quickly. They did not preach ideas from the Bible; they acted out the Bible.
>
> We were all being tuned to God and what He wanted to do. We did not waste motion but seemed to be carried into effectiveness, seeing God act. All were excited and fully engaged. The atmosphere was electric. We seemed so different. We knew what to do. We knew how to pray and share accurately and see God move. God, in fact, moved us as we witnessed His work in our lives or quoted Scripture. We had a calmness and resolve yet were very vital and alive. We knew He was directing us and followed His direction without hesitation. He was part of everything. We were full of His presence. We didn't talk of His presence as something unusual, but embraced it as normal. No one wasted time or words, but everything carried power and effect. It was like everything we had read and known about God and the Bible was actually happening in our lives, and we were sharing as the Spirit

highlighted things.

It was a hundred times more powerful than a normal church meeting. God was everywhere. Everyone was serious yet joyful. Some were farther along and were sharing how God was moving in order to encourage others. Faith filled the room. Everyone had that look of faith and intensity in their eyes. The feel of the atmosphere was nearly impossible to describe. God was so strong on us, yet we were not behaving as a group of nice committed Christians; we were radically given over to God. We had moved to a new level. 'God' was with us tangibly, yet we were so natural, purposeful, and directed. God's presence had given us a whole new sense of life and how to behave.

Prayer, prophesying, praise and exhortation seemed to merge into one. We were doing it all without separation or definition. It came spontaneously and ordered. There was no confusion. The anointing was on everyone. God permeated everything. He spoke through different ones just as they were; they were being themselves. Not everyone spoke, but everyone was completely engaged. We felt close to each other. There was no time or place for pettiness or silly divisions. We were open to receive from each other as natural as breathing. No one dominated. No one actually led, though those who had been through more shared more and with a richness and quality that caused everyone to listen and receive. No one was bored or wanted to leave. No one tried to upstage anyone else. The Presence of God coordinated everything, and everything was appropriate. He was the plan. He was the order. No other coordination or plan was necessary. We all felt motivated and excited as we were leaving, both for our lives and everyone else in the group. Love was everywhere!!!

Chapter 29
Activity #3: Financially Caring for Each Other

Acts 2:44-45 (NASB): And all those who had believed were together and had all things in common; and they began selling their property and possessions and were sharing them with all, as anyone might have need.

Generosity among believers is a sign of their sincere love for each other. It's a sign of healthy fellowship. It's the result of the Gospel getting down into the hearts of people by the Spirit, Jesus the Messiah being made real to them. It's love in action:

I Jn 3:16-19 (NKJ): By this we know love, because He laid down His life for us. And we also ought to lay down our lives for the brethren. But whoever has this world's goods, and sees his brother in need, and shuts up his heart from him, how does the love of God abide in him? My little children, let us not love in word or in tongue, but in deed and in truth. And by this we know that we are of the truth, and shall assure our hearts before Him.

Rom 12:9, 13 (NKJ): Let love be without hypocrisy. Abhor what is evil. Cling to what is good...[be] distributing to the needs of the saints, given to hospitality.

Regarding the Corinthian disciples' giving, Paul said,

2 Cor 8:8 (NKJ): ...I am testing the sincerity of your love.

Giving to the needy among us is a litmus test of sincere Christian love. It's how we know that we're not meeting for merely selfish purposes.

In the Legislatures of many cities today, much poverty would be alleviated among us if we lived like the early disciples. The rich would care for the poorer believers' legitimate needs. We see this radical generosity among God's People not only in Jerusalem but among Legislatures elsewhere also:

2 Cor 8:13-14 (NKJ): For I do not mean that others should be eased and you burdened; but by an equality, that now at this time your abundance may supply their lack, that their abundance also may supply your lack—that there may be equality.

This kind of generosity can't be produced by an outward law or tradition forced down on people. It's a grace (2Cor 8:1, 7). It must be responded to. It comes through the work of the Gospel in our hearts by the Spirit. Paul said about giving, "I speak not by commandment" (2Cor 8:8). He also said not to give under compulsion (2Cor 9:7). We're all to grow in generosity by *grace*. The New Covenant works by the Spirit from the inside out. It involves a process that takes varying amounts of time. Therefore, no specific amount of money should be imposed on believers to give, though they should be challenged upward by through the Word. Leaders are to ensure *truths* about giving and generosity are taught, which the Spirit writes on believers' hearts. Then they are to stand back and watch to see what kind of grace the believers have received by their resulting actions.

Also leaders have a responsibility to not tie up believers' funds so much in unprofitable projects that they can't use their money to help the poor and fund outreach.

There was a conference in my city in which many offerings were taken. The people seemed worn out from it after a while. So when an announcement was made that a special offering for single mothers was going to be taken up, the man who made it didn't expect much. However, to his surprise the offering bags were filled to overflowing! Believers who love God want to give to the needy among them. Leaders need to facilitate that desire and require less for buildings in many cases. Traditional-churches in the US alone spend over $10 billion per year on buildings.[23]

Legislatures in Acts took care of widows and others in need:

1 Tim 5:16 (NKJ): ...If any believing man or woman has widows, let them relieve them, and do not let the [Legislature] be burdened, that it may relieve those who are really widows.

James 1:27 (NKJ): Pure and undefiled religion before God and the Father is this: to visit orphans and widows in their trouble, and to keep oneself unspotted from the world.

When the Legislature in Acts "began selling their property and possessions and were sharing them with all, as anyone might have need," God absolutely loved it. It was so much of a beautiful thing in Heaven that Satan inspired Ananias and Sapphira to mess it up. Because they knowingly collaborated with Satan to do it, God killed them. He would not let the purity of such beautiful offerings and fellowship be tainted.

When this aspect of Christianity becomes common in Legislatures, the world will see it and be amazed. Their attention will be grabbed when they see that we value Jesus and each other more than money. Their carnal minds will be shocked. They'll know we're not lying. And the way of the world, "Lust of the eyes, lust of the body, and the boasting of what man has and does" (1Jn 2:16), will be broken in us. As we give freely, we contradict it. We're putting the ax to the root of the tree. And we're paving the way to make future sacrifices which will be

---

[23] David Platt, *Radical* (Colorado Springs, CO: Multnomah Books, 2010), 118.

required of us to take hold of the Kingdom in the next age:

1 Tim 6:17-19 (NASB): Instruct those who are rich in this present world not to be conceited or to fix their hope on the uncertainty of riches, but on God, who richly supplies us with all things to enjoy. Instruct them to do good, to be rich in good works, to be generous and ready to share, storing up for themselves the treasure of a good foundation for the future, so that they may take hold of that which is life indeed.

Finally, giving physical gifts to each other is part of our priestly ministry. While blessing others with giving, we are also blessing God.

Heb 13:16 (NKJ): But do not forget to do good and to share, for with such sacrifices God is well pleased.

Phil 4:18 (NKJ): Indeed I have all and abound. I am full, having received from Epaphroditus the things sent from you, a sweet-smelling aroma, an acceptable sacrifice, well pleasing to God...

Chapter 30
Activity #4: Prayer, Praise, & Other Priestly Offerings

Acts 2:42 (NASB): They were continually devoting themselves to the apostles' teaching and to fellowship, to the breaking of bread *and to prayer.*

Acts 2:46-47 (NASB): Day by day continuing with one mind *in the temple...praising God...*

Another activity this pattern Legislature continually devoted itself to was prayer. Additionally, verse 46 shows they spent time in the temple, which meant they were also thanking, praising, and worshiping God. All of these are part of the priestly aspect of our new nature:

1 Pet 2:9 (NKJ): ...you are a chosen generation, a royal priesthood, a holy nation, His own special people, that you may proclaim the praises of Him who called you out of darkness into His marvelous light.

Rev 1:5-6 (NKJ): ...Jesus Christ...loved us and washed us from our sins in His own blood, and has made us kings and priests to His God and Father...

The Bible declares all believers to be priests now through the New Covenant. As such we have duties to perform before God. Specifically, priests *offer sacrifices.* The sacrifices we offer are acceptable to God through our High Priest, Jesus:

1 Pet 2:5 (NKJ): ...as living stones, [you] are being built up a spiritual house, a holy priesthood, to offer up spiritual sacrifices acceptable to God through Jesus Christ.

What are these sacrifices we're to offer today? The first and most fundamental offering, in view of Jesus' cross, is our physical bodies—laying them down completely on God's alter:

Rom 12:1 (NKJ): I beseech you therefore, brethren, by the mercies of God, that you present your bodies a living sacrifice, holy, acceptable to God, which is your reasonable [priestly] service.

We also looked at the offering of financial giving in the last chapter. The following are more of what we as New Covenant priests are to offer.

- Thanksgiving (Ps 50:14)
- Praise (Ps 50:23, Heb 13:15)
- Prayers, supplications (requests for mercy) and intercession (Heb 5:7, 7:25-26; Ac 12:5; Ps 141:2)

These are various aspects of "ministering to the Lord," a term used in Acts 13:2. Ministering to the Lord is to be done both individually and corporately. Acts 2:46 says they were "with one mind in the temple." They were unified. It's a blessing to be able to offer these sacrifices to God collectively:

Rom 15:5-6 (NKJ): Now may the God of patience and comfort grant you to be like-minded toward one another, according to Christ Jesus, that you may with *one mind and one mouth* glorify the God and Father of our Lord Jesus Christ.

The "one mouth" here may specifically refer to singing praise songs together. Of course, all of the sacrifices can be offered with or without music, as long as they're on the foundation of the first offering of our whole selves. And music is a wonderful tool which can be used to facilitate thanksgiving, praise, and worship. The hymn the disciples and Jesus sang the last time they were together before he was crucified must have been charged with the Spirit (Mt 26:30). It must have stayed with them the rest of their lives. Our singing today, with and for Jesus, can be the same:

Heb 2:12 (NKJ): "I [Jesus] will declare Your name to My brethren; In the midst of the [Royal] assembly I will sing praise to You."

Paul instructed disciples to utilize three specific tools of praise & thanksgiving in at least some of their meetings: psalms, hymns, and spiritual songs (Eph 5:19, Col 3:16).

Teaching must be provided for believers on praise and what it means to "magnify the Lord." This way, people will better understand why they're singing and what's happening as they make these offerings. Also, just as with giving, the amount of Good News people have received will affect their ability to make each of these offerings.

There is a correlation between our priestly duties and the exercise of our kingly authority. For example, through prayer we can rule on Earth. It is a powerful weapon, listed in Ephesians as the spear in our armor—in modern language, the long range missile or even intercontinental ballistic missile (atom-bomb):

Ephesians 6:18 (NASB): With all prayer and petition pray at all times in the Spirit, and with this in view, be on the alert with all perseverance and petition for all the saints…

We also exercise our kingly authority by spiritual proclamations, made through the Spirit. We perform our priestly ministry upward and eventually God extends the rod of Jesus Christ through us into the earth (Ps 110:1-2). So as we perform our priestly duties, we should be ready, standing by to use the spiritual, double-edged sword on the earth:

Ps 149:5-9 (NKJ): Let the saints be joyful in glory; let them sing aloud on their beds. Let the high praises of God be in their mouth, and a two-edged sword in their hand, To execute vengeance on the nations, and punishments on the peoples; To bind their kings with chains, and their nobles with fetters of iron; To execute on them the written judgment—this honor have all His saints. Praise the LORD!

We see this powerful sword operating as the Legislature in Jerusalem, "offered constant prayer to God for Peter" when he was put in jail to be executed (Ac 12:5). The result was release for him by the angel of the Lord and eventually the death of Herod by the same angel.

They "were continually devoting themselves...to prayer":

Acts 3:1 (NKJ): Now Peter and John went up together to the temple at the hour of prayer, the ninth hour.

Acts 16:13 (NKJ): And on the Sabbath day we went out of the city to the riverside, where prayer was customarily made; and we sat down...

Rom 12:12 (NKJ): ...continue steadfastly in prayer...

Colossians 4:2 (NASB): Devote yourselves to prayer, keeping alert in it with [thanksgiving]...

Paul instructed Timothy to set up prayer meetings, "first of all," and they were to include prayer for government officials:

1 Tim 2:1-4 (NASB): First of all, then, I urge that entreaties and prayers, petitions and thanksgivings, be made on behalf of all men, for kings and all who are in authority, so that we may lead a tranquil and quiet life in all godliness and dignity. This is good and acceptable in the sight of God our Savior, who desires all men to be saved and to come to the knowledge of the truth.

I suppose one test to see if we're more a part of the traditional-church form or the original one is if corporate prayer is the first priority of our meetings and if we include prayer for government leaders. I ask you, the reader, to examine yourself: when was the last time you prayed with a group of believers for government officials? Among most of us this is very rare. I think it should become a regular part of our meetings, or at least our prayer meetings, which should also become regular.

What would happen if we, through reform, begin implementing prayer for leaders and "all men," people from all walks of life—government, occult practitioners, pornographers, atheist God-haters, Hollywood actors, educators, business leaders, people trapped in false religions...? They would "be saved," as the verse says. No doubt, prayer like this is part of why some of them have been saved. Corporate prayer needs to become a regular part of Christian life again, and we need to grow in how to do it, by the Spirit and the Word. We will become a powerful force.

There is an annual, "International Day of Prayer for The Persecuted Church" ("IDOP"). An organization that works with persecuted believers around the world reported that after that day of prayer the struggling believers under persecution very evidently received relief. What if it becomes once a week? The world will be shaken just as in the first century when God's priests continually devoted themselves to prayer (Ac 2:42).[24]

Another aspect of prayer is for the establishment of new disciples. Many prayers are required to help them grow to maturity. Here are a few examples of this:

Col 4:12-13 (NKJ): Epaphras, who is one of you, a bondservant of Christ, greets you, always laboring fervently for you in prayers, that you may stand perfect and complete in all the will of God. For I bear him witness that he has a great zeal for you, and those who are in Laodicea,

---

[24] I recommend this prayer tool: *The Persecuted Church Global Report 2011*, by The Voice of the Martyrs.

and those in Hierapolis.

2 Cor 13:7, 9 (NKJ): Now I pray to God that you do no evil...And this also we pray, that you may be made complete.

Phil 1:9 (NKJ): And this I pray, that your love may abound still more and more...

Col 1:9 (NKJ): [We] do not cease to pray for you, and to ask that you may be filled with the knowledge of His will...

2 Thes 1:11 (NKJ): Therefore we also pray always for you that our God would count you worthy of this calling...

Acts also records *fasting* done along with prayer. Fasting amplifies prayer. It was done corporately and individually. Instructions are given by Jesus and throughout the Word on how to do it. It's another activity we *absolutely* need to re-implement. And it must be done accurately, not blindly.

We often think of the early apostles as very powerful people who accomplished a lot in their time and generation. We shouldn't overlook the fact that a major force behind their ministries was the prayer of Legislatures already in existence. The apostles were very dependent on it:

2 Cor 1:10-11 (NASB): [God who raises the dead] delivered us from so great a peril of death, and will deliver us—He on whom we have set our hope. And He will yet deliver us, *you also joining in helping us through your prayers*, so that thanks may be given by many persons on our behalf for the favor bestowed on us through the prayers of many.

Phil 1:19 (NKJ): For I know that this will turn out for my deliverance [from prison] through your prayer and the supply of the Spirit of Jesus Christ...

Col 4:2-4 (NKJ): Continue earnestly in prayer, being vigilant in it with thanksgiving; meanwhile praying also for us, that God would open to us a door for the word, to speak the mystery of Christ, for which I am also in chains, that I may make it manifest, as I ought to speak.

2 Thes 3:1-2 (NKJ): Finally, brethren, pray for us, that the word of the Lord may run swiftly and be glorified, just as it is with you, and that we may be delivered from unreasonable and wicked men; for not all have faith.

Notice that as they prayed, doors were open to Paul's team to spread the Gospel. The Gospel and prayer work closely together. The twelve apostles said at one point,

Acts 6:4 (NKJ): "...we will give ourselves continually to prayer and to the ministry of the word."

I mentioned that in our armor, prayer is the spear (or long range missile) of the Spirit. Speaking the Word is the sword (or handgun) of the Spirit.

Eph 6:17 (NKJ): And take...the sword of the Spirit, which is the word [Gr., "spoken word"] of God...

The two offensive weapons of *speaking God's word* and *prayer* must go together. Using the spear and the sword are limited to each other. Without prayer, a door may not open to go with the Gospel. Without actually going to people and speaking to them, people can't hear the Good News and believe. So prayer is meant to support the work of the Great Commission.

For this reason, even if a Legislature is receiving enough teaching, having fellowship, eating the Lord's Supper and other meals with honesty and sincerity, being generous to each other in love, and praying together, it is still incomplete without the next and final activity listed in Acts 2: evangelistic outreach. We'll cover this in the next chapter.

Chapter 31
Activity #5: Evangelism

Acts 2:47 (NASB): ...And the Lord was adding to their number day by day those who were being saved.

We see here that daily people were being born again. This means daily people were witnessing of Jesus (Rom 10:10-14). The basis on which these believers evangelized was their known identity, stated by Jesus earlier:

Acts 1:8 (NASB): You will receive power when the Holy Spirit has come upon you; and you shall be My witnesses...to the remotest part of the earth."

Each believer, at that time, saw himself or herself as a witness of Jesus. It was their identity, given to them by the Lord, and with it came the responsibility to testify to others about Jesus. There was no such thing as a believer that was not also a witness of Jesus. They weren't called Christians at that time. They all knew of themselves as Jesus' witnesses and acted accordingly. They all evangelized:

Acts 8:1, 4 (NKJ): At that time a great persecution arose against the church which was at Jerusalem; and they were all scattered throughout the regions of Judea and Samaria, except the apostles...Therefore those who were scattered went everywhere preaching the word ["carrying the Good News to people"].

If we view the Body of Christ as a great iceberg, evangelism is the part emerging out of the water. This is why I've listed it last out of these five essential activities. It's also listed last in Acts 2. The other activities, generally unseen by the world, are the weight and force behind our outreach. They also provide an environment for new converts to grow up in.

Notice that *"the Lord was adding"* them. If we get these other aspects of Biblical Christianity in place, the LORD HIMSELF will add people to us. So putting the other activities in place is perhaps the greatest preparation for evangelism.

Evangelism is invigorating because of the propelling power of the Holy Spirit. It allows the River of God to flow through us to a lost, hurting world (Jn 4:14, 7:38). It helps us stay clear on the difference between us and the world. It also builds stronger relationships among us as we go out together, as the Lord instructed (Mt 10; Lk 10).

The Gospels document the *outreach* of Jesus and his team and also include the *further development* he gave them along the way. After Jesus left, Acts primarily documents the *outreach* of believers in Jesus, whereas the Epistles were written primarily as *further development* for them. To complete the will of God, according to the Great Commission, we need to have both.

Presently, ministry in much of the world seems to consist of about 99% ritual and development, and 1% outreach. One reform we need to make is to include both outreach *and* development in the lives of every believer. This includes both *defense* and *offense*. No war or competition can be won without offense. If we don't have the offense of outreach, we will definitely lose.

King David's great fall with Bathsheba obviously started with David staying home and not going out to battle (2Sam 11:1). He decided to relax a bit, when it wasn't time to do so. That's what opened him up to fall. Many of us are falling in similar ways. We need to know that the reason is *not* because of an inherent moral problem in us. "No temptation has come against us that's not common to man" (1Cor 10:13). In many cases, it's the result of a structural issue. A major aspect of our Christianity is missing. We all, to varying degrees and in varying ways, need to be involved in outreach.

To make this shift will bring an experience of Christian victory many have hardly tasted. It will alleviate a multitude of our problems. Many of the problems we struggle to fix—in ourselves and in those we lead—will be fixed by the Lord himself if we make this shift.

Participating in evangelism—50% of the Great Commission—is wise because it ensures freedom from unnecessary temptations, and it carries *great* reward upon Jesus' return.

Outreach allows people to go beyond their pressing circumstances or problems they perceive as giants. They choose to not look at their personal problems but to *act* on the truths they've received, in order to help others. In the process, those reached are helped and those doing the outreach are too. The Spirit as living rivers flows out of their belly, as they speak, and cleanses them and those they speak to (John 7:38).

Outreach is one way to "seek first God's Kingdom," so it enables God to "add all we need unto us" (Mt 6:33). Outreach also lets us use his power; it's one of the places signs, wonders, miracles, and gifts of the Spirit are found, aligned with God's will (Heb 2:4). Once trained, much of a disciple's sustenance will come as he's serving. Various miracles he or she needs will be waiting on the other side of stepping out and giving.

As Jesus said, we should freely give as we've freely received (Mt 10:8). If we've received a spiritual truth, we need at some point to give it to someone else. If we've been given a spiritual gift, we need to use it for others as we have opportunity. If we don't, we'll lose our ability to keep receiving. If we're serving, we'll need a continuous flow from God and he'll surely give it:

Prov 11:25 (NKJ): The generous soul will be made rich, and he who waters will also be watered himself.

Luke 6:38 (NKJ): Give, and it will be given to you...

2 Cor 9:10: (NKJ): [God] supplies seed to the *sower*...

Looking into the Epistles can give us only snapshots of the activities of the New Testament Legislatures. They were teaching letters, not meant to document the outreach going on at the time. We have the Book of Acts for that, which is what those who received the Epistles *were living at the time*. That said, even in the Epistles we can see that outreach was basic and assumed for believers. Consider the following:

Phil 1:27-28 (NKJ): Only let your conduct be worthy of the gospel of Christ, so that whether I come and see you or am absent, I may hear of your affairs, that you stand fast in one spirit, with one mind *striving together for the faith of the gospel*, and not in any way terrified by your adversaries...

Eph 6:15 (NKJ): ...and having shod your feet with the preparation [to march out with] the gospel of peace...

1 Cor 15:58 (NKJ): Therefore, my beloved brethren, be steadfast, immovable, always *abounding in the work of the Lord*, knowing that your labor is not in vain in the Lord.

These early believers were united in fulfilling the Great Commission the Lord left us. Paul wrote to help them stay united and persevering in this work.

Other verses in the Epistles show that the first believers evangelized and began training disciples in most or all of their known world (Rom 15:20-23, Col 1:6). This could not have been done by apostles and evangelists alone. Those who were evangelized also evangelized (see Ac 13:48-49, Mk 16:15-20).

Not all new converts are alike. Some new disciples are ready to immediately evangelize others based on the surge of the Good News they received. In those cases, such zeal needs to be maintained. Elders and all believers need to maintain an environment for zealous new converts in which they do not have to turn their fire down to relate to older believers. Some other new believers will not be given that level of zeal immediately. However, they can be trained and develop zeal over time, according to the particular grace God gives them.

Some new converts will be so charged they can evangelize whole neighborhoods in the first few months of being born again. However, though a fire has been lit and new believers are burning, it must be understood that they are not ready for much teaching or shepherding responsibility in the Legislature (1Tim 3:6, 5:22). They are in the stage of being ministered to, as baby Christians. Their minds haven't been renewed much yet, and they haven't been proved.

I heard a teacher in the Body of Christ relate something the Lord revealed to him about Christian growth and service:

1. First we get to *know* God
2. Then we learn thereby to *trust* God
3. Then we will *love* God
4. Then out of that, we naturally *serve* God[25]

We need to be careful not to get this order reversed. Often believers who haven't developed a relationship with God are put prematurely into positions of leadership because of their evident gifts or talents. But the challenges they face can cause them to fall if they haven't been equipped thoroughly. They have to get to know, trust and love God first.

Philippians 1:27-28, quoted above, shows that in the face of adversaries, the early disciples worked together to get the Gospel out and believed on. In the same context, Paul stated he was happy to have been put in prison because his example encouraged many believers to evangelize more boldly:

Phil 1:12-14 (NIV): Now I want you to know, brothers, that what has happened to me has really served to advance the gospel. As a result, it has become clear throughout the whole palace guard and to everyone else that I am in chains for Christ. Because of my chains, most of the brothers in the Lord have been encouraged to speak the

---

[25] Ed Glaspey, Doug Easterday, Linda Frizzell, Jane Akeson, and Dan Wallis, *Restoration School* (Junction City, OR), DVD & Audio CD.

word of God more courageously and fearlessly.

A leader who went to the United States after experiencing horrible persecuted in Romania under the USSR wrote a powerful book about the persecuted Christians there. He documented their work of spreading the Good News despite laws and brutal consequences against it. He stated, "We should never stop at having won a soul for Christ. By this, you have done only *half* the work. Every soul won for Christ must be made to be a soul-winner."[26] If that could be the norm in a country where they'd likely go to prison or worse for spreading the Gospel, how much more should it be the norm for us in freer countries? We need to bring the outreach factor of Christianity back among us.

Matt 5:13-15 (NASB): You are the salt of the earth…You are the light of the world. A city set on a hill cannot be hidden; nor does anyone light a lamp and put it under a basket, but on the lampstand, and it gives light to all who are in the house.

---

[26] Richard Wurmbrand *Tortured For Christ* (Bartlesville, OK: Living Sacrifice Book Company, 1967), 28. (Free copy now available from torturedforchrist.com).

Chapter 32
The Result of the Combination of These Activities

Acts 2:43 (NKJ): Then fear came upon every soul, and many wonders and signs were done through the apostles.

Fear came on every soul. This indicates the presence of God was manifested. His miraculous power also was shown at that time through the apostles—those with more training and capacity to hold it. God and King Jesus were glorified.

This was not a unique or one-time thing. As the believers continued meeting the various conditions, this wonder from God was maintained among Legislatures in every location:

Acts 9:31 (NKJ): Then the [Legislatures] throughout all Judea, Galilee, and Samaria had peace and were edified. And walking in the fear of the Lord and in the comfort of the Holy Spirit, they were multiplied.

Although "all endurance" will be required, power, wonder, glory, joy, peace, and other benefits of the New Covenant are always intended to increase (2Cor 3:7-18). By Acts 4, persecution broke out against these believers, but they continued doing all these right things—so the power and glory of God among them increased. However, as we know, the Legislature eventually stopped meeting the conditions necessary to enjoy the glory of God manifested, so it was lost. Now we have an opportunity to go back to the original way and receive it again.

By re-implementing these five essential activities, which are provisions for God's People, God's glory will be revealed, for us and through us.

Chapter 33
Gifts in Every Legislature
(Restoring Full Participation to our Main Meetings)

The reformation of structure I'm encouraging will result in many gifts operating in every Legislature. In this chapter, I cover over 20 distinct "gifts" in Scripture. Currently, many of these do not operate regularly, simply because of the lack of opportunity to minister in meetings. Many of the most mature and refined believers we have, because they did not go to seminary or take on the role of traditional pastor, are relegated to a seat, to sit and listen. The powerful gifts and weapons in them are not utilized. Instead, they must listen to material they've learned, lived, and sometimes taught for years. Of course we *all* need teaching, but there's also a need to not go back to the elementary things.

As we utilize the format in Acts, which we've looked at extensively, those empowered to teach can teach. Those who can lead teams or mentor will naturally do so. People's gifts will make room for them, as God intended.

This will greatly benefit people who travel and evangelize or teach. Often in their hometowns they can't use their gifts. They're not appreciated and can't even tell others what they've done on their travels (very different than what we see, e.g., in Acts 14:27-28). They don't get the needed relational support from others because of so little fellowship in the traditional meeting. They get bored. Then they face the danger of falling as King David did because of the inactivity. Or they have to run their difficult race in isolation. Reformation will allow them a place to serve while not traveling; they'll be able to contribute to the Legislature where they live. It will also allow them to make stabilizing relationships. The fellowship involved will be to them like a refreshing glass of water. They'll be able to refuel and get healed from any wounds suffered at battle.

Furthermore, reformation of our format will allow the gifts God puts in every Legislature to rise up among us. They will arise from within the most seemingly unlikely people. For example, every Legislature is to have the regular use of "gifts of healings" (1Cor 12:28). This was true of the New Testament Legislatures, even when they were temporarily off track morally or doctrinally. Miracles were worked regularly among believers in Galatia (Gal 3:5). Corinth also had various gifts that were regularly used, including workings of miracles and gifts of healings (1Cor 12:28).

Currently, the gifts that function are almost exclusively through a regular speaker or traveling ministries. Please don't get me wrong; in many cases this has done *much* good. Thank God for that. Thank God. But many more gifts are available that we are not utilizing.

To look into this, let's first consider the following:

1 Cor 12:1, 4-6 (NASB): Now concerning spiritual [things], brethren, I do not want you to be unaware [or, "ignorant"]…there are varieties of gifts, but the same Spirit. And there are varieties of ministries, and the same Lord. There are varieties of effects [or, "workings"], but the same God who works all things *in all persons*.

A gift is something that is free and unmerited. Because of this, we can *ALL* be used in meetings. Gifts are not earned but received from God, for the benefit of others. They are supernatural and come from God's generosity.

There's a stronghold in many of our minds that gifts are limiting. But gifts are not given to exclude, but in order to include all of us. If you've wondered why they're so scarce among us, I'll tell you one reason in a moment.

First though, let me share more about gifts. Some gifts in

Scripture are like jobs; they are services. Ephesians 4:8-11 speaks of five "gifts," which Jesus gave to equip others: apostle, prophet, evangelist, shepherd, and teacher (we covered these in Part 4). I believe all of us, as we grow, may fill these equipping roles, though the Lord chooses which exactly. These can be referred to as the "equipping gifts."

These are the kind of gifts that we receive, sometimes through the laying on of hands, sometimes accompanied by prophecy and revelation. This kind of gift is permanently given (Romans 11:29) and can be neglected. As Paul told Timothy,

1Timothy 4:14 (NKJV): Do not neglect the gift that is in you, which was given to you by prophecy with the laying on of the hands of the eldership."

2Timothy 1:6 (NIV): I remind you to fan into flame the gift of God, which is in you through the laying on of my hands.

These are jobs that we can be "appointed for" by God (2Tim 1:11). Paul, for example, had the gifts of evangelist, apostle, and teacher (1Tim 2:7). He also had a supernatural gift of celibacy (1Cor 7:7).

However, there is another kind of "gift" in Scripture. These are simply things that we give to one another when we meet in a full participation setting (see 1Peter 4:10-11). We don't own these. What has been called, "the manifestation of the Spirit," (1Cor 12:7) or "gifts of the Spirit" (1Cor 12:4), work this way, as I see it.

Now let me point out something I recently discovered about "the manifestation of the Spirit," which has changed my thinking completely on the subject. First, "manifestation" is better translated, "exhibition," "expression," or *"presentation."* Second, the word for "common good," is "symphero." It has two clear meanings: "to profit," and "to bring together." It's used in Acts 19:19 when they "brought together all the books...." Here, in the context of Body parts, each with various functions that come together to make a whole, this word clearly should be translated, "to bring together." So the verse should read:

1 Cor 12:7: However, to each one is given a presentation, [by the] Spirit, in order to bring all together.

This truth must be seen in the practical context of New Testament full participation meetings:

1 Cor 14:26: When you come together, each of you has a psalm, has a teaching, has a tongue, has a revelation, an interpretation....

We are each given, by the Spirit, a presentation in the meeting, something to share with the rest of the Body. The fact that traditional meetings don't utilize this provision doesn't change it. There are multitudes of presentations that *we are missing* because of our meeting format's lack of room for this.

This also shows that in New Testament meetings, the Spirit is relied on primarily because our presentations consist of sharing gifts put in us by Him (1Pe 4:10). The Spirit gives the following gifts to various people, for their presentation:

1 Cor 12:7-12: A presentation of the Spirit is given to each one to bring all together. For to one is given the word [or, "message"] of wisdom through the Spirit, and to another the word [or, "message"] of knowledge according to the same Spirit; to another faith by the same Spirit, and to another gifts of healings by the one Spirit, and to another the workings of miracles, and to another prophecy, and to another the discerning of spirits, to another various kinds of tongues [or, "varieties of supernatural languages"], and to another the [supernatural] interpretation of tongues [i.e., "languages"]. But one and the same Spirit works all these things, distributing *to each one* individually just as He wills. Just as a body, though one, has many parts, but all its many parts form one body, so it is with Christ.

The Spirit distributes them as He wills. Therefore He's in control. He's in the driver's seat. He is to be leading.

We can't control who will get which gifts to give each meeting, but we can know that it's the Spirit's will to distribute them, so we can look for them and cooperate with Him. We can position ourselves for them (1Cor 12:11, Heb 2:4) and ask for them with expectancy (1Cor 12:31, Lk 11:5-13).

Here's information on each of these nine gifts:

1. <u>A message of wisdom</u>—communication of wisdom from the Spirit, received through the spiritual senses
2. <u>A message of knowledge</u>—received through the spiritual senses; can be knowledge about anything past, present, or future
3. <u>Faith</u>—the use of faith by command "moves mountains" (1Cor 13:2, Mk 11:23). For some things, faith is used through prayer (Mk 11:24). It's used to fix problems
4. <u>Gifts of healings</u>—I believe this is simply a New Testament term used for supernatural healing. Healings are free "gifts" that we give to others. They're freely given. These are plural, so it's not that a person has "a special gifting of being able to heal people." We all can heal, through the Authority of Jesus, by faith. We are passing on a gift, a present, freely given by God to a person in need. In a meeting context, it can be used by some people present, but there are many other things that God wants to take place in a meeting also
5. <u>Workings of Miracles</u>—distinct from healing; as I see it, this would include re-creating body parts, for example, stopping storms, and any other miracle needed
6. <u>Prophecy</u>—speaking a specific message from God; can be about past, present, or future; 2Pe 1:20-21: "...no prophecy of Scripture is a matter of one's own interpretation, for no prophecy was ever made by an act of human will, but men moved by the Holy Spirit spoke from God." Among other benefits, prophecy gives God's People, "edification, exhortation, and comfort"

(1Cor 14:3). This was emphasized by Paul as a presentation to primarily seek, for the edification of others in the meeting
7. Discerning of spirits—information given by the Holy Spirit about spirits: primarily evil spirits and angels. In a meeting, this would be useful for the identifying of evil spirits to deal with that are present, or for prayer and spiritual warfare, for example. If given to you, making it known and/or acting on it is your presentation in that meeting
8. Various languages (or "diverse tongues")—These are given specifically by the Spirit, in addition to the unknown language you receive through Holy Spirit immersion. (That language you can use by your will anytime—Acts 2:38-39, 1Cor 14:15). These can effect powerful changes and can also convey a message to be interpreted. In a meeting, a supernatural language is to be interpreted, for everyone's edification. The message may be praise to God, giving of thanks, a message from God, spiritual warfare...
9. Interpretation of languages—supernatural. Can be done by the one who spoke the tongue or by someone else; in public we're told to pray for an interpretation (1Cor 14:13), with faith and expectation (Jas 1:6-7). Paul gives instructions on how to do this in chapter 14, which I will highlight later on

To use and enjoy these spiritual gifts, reliance on the Holy Spirit is required. We must gain knowledge about them (1Cor 12:1), zealously seek them (1Cor 12:31, 14:1) have a format that promotes the use of them; and grow in learning to use them. The reason these gifts are so scarce is because of ignorance about them, lack of desire for them, and our traditional meeting format, which doesn't allow for them!

The Spirit can give one or more of these gifts to any disciple he wants, whenever he wants. He spreads them out among a group in order to involve everyone. However, never think you can only utilize one or that each person only receives one. 1Corinthians 13 describes one person potentially utilizing all of them, which is very normal. Several places in the Bible give examples of people utilizing several of them, including the Lord Jesus, our example. Plus they often work together.

It's true that anyone can receive and give these, by the Spirit. But in a meeting, they're distributed "to each one" as the Spirit chooses. No one person can do them all and deprive the others of their presentation. The Spirit gives something to present, to *each one*.

After covering these presentations or "gifts" of the Spirit, given to each one, Paul calls each participant a member of Jesus' risen Body. He emphasizes the variety and equality of each part and the *necessity* of each one (see 1Cor 12:12-27).

Since there are many needs to be met, and in order to bring us all together as Jesus' functioning Body, the Spirit will only use some people to work miracles in a meeting, for example. Someone else will share a message of knowledge, for example. Otherwise, "where would the Body be?" (1Cor 12:19).

Now let's look at the picture in Romans of the Body coming together and using various gifts for mutual edification:

Rom 12:3-8 (NASB): For through the grace given to me I say to everyone among you not to think more highly of himself than he ought to think; but to think so as to have sound judgment, as God has allotted to each a measure of faith. For just as we have many members in one body and all the members do not have the same function, so we, who are many, are one body in Christ, and individually members one of another. Since we have gifts that differ according to the grace given to us, each of us is to exercise them accordingly: if <u>prophecy</u>, according to the proportion of his faith; if <u>service</u> [Gr., diakonia], in his serving; or <u>he who teaches</u>, in his teaching; or <u>he who exhorts</u> [I.e., "encourages forward"], in his exhortation; <u>he who gives</u>, with liberality [or, "with sincere simplicity,"]; <u>he who leads</u> [Gr., proistemi, "to stand before"], with diligence; <u>he who shows mercy</u> [or, "compassion"], with cheerfulness.

Gifts listed here that are not covered above:

1. Service—this word has a broad use in Scripture. Here I believe it refers to non-speaking gifts, such as "gifts of healings," and "workings of miracles." I believe so because of 1Peter 4:10-11, which breaks gifts into two general categories of speaking and of "serving," to be done "in the power God supplies":

1 Pet 4:10-11 (NKJ): As *each one* has received a gift, minister it to one another, as good stewards of the manifold grace of God. If *anyone* speaks, let him speak as the oracles of God. If *anyone* ministers ["serves"], let him do it as with the ability which God supplies, that in all things God may be glorified through Jesus Christ…

2. Teaching—pretty straightforward, but note that in the main-meeting format, it's a gift that anyone can bring to a meeting:

1 Cor 14:26 (NKJ): Whenever you come together, *each of you* has a psalm, has a teaching, has a tongue, has a revelation, an interpretation. Let all things be done for edification.

3. Exhortation (or, "encouraging forward")
4. Giving (financially)—In addition to regular giving each disciple should be built up to, the Spirit will work in people to give financially in a specific, special way
5. Leading—given for the two leadership roles revealed in Scripture: apostles and elders,[27] to those leading a team, or to anyone else leading. The Spirit helps them in their leading
6. Showing mercy (or, "compassion")

All can do each of these things at times, but the Spirit will

---

[27] Page 20 has a list of 10 aspects of Elders' leadership, and the work of apostles is described in chapter 21

give each person these gifts in order to bring all together as the completely functioning Body of Christ. The instruction in Romans 12, above, is to do what God is giving you at the time, and to be sure to recognize that God gives a measure of faith to *each person*, so we all need each other's contributions. The gifts work by faith, so you should do what you have faith to do at the time. If you see that you can do something, just do it.

If you're not sure what you can contribute, ask the Lord for something. If you're still unsure, wait on the Lord, then try something. The Spirit will give you something to contribute, as Jesus desires to use his whole Body. Love others and seek to edify them, while being respectful and not taking up time allotted to others, and you can't fail (1Cor 13:8).

From meeting to meeting, who is used in what way will change. Use the gift you're given at the time, during that meeting. If you notice a pattern, feel free to go with it, being careful not to try to put the Spirit in a box or limit each other. The Spirit gives various things as he sees fit, so we are dependent on Him. We must keep our eyes on Him and what He wants to do. He's gentle, and we will have to launch out with our presentations, depending on him. What you think you can do at the time, while relying on Him, you can likely do, with proper boundaries of respect for others and minding the time. Like everything in the life of faith, we all grow in this by doing.

To receive and use gifts simply requires an environment to serve one another. In some cases, we've limited ourselves, unsure if we "have" a certain gift. But they're not limiting; we can serve, according to what we believe we can do, and as we simply do so, we will find ourselves using grace in us (i.e., giving gifts). Don't feel limited; always do what is in front of you, in love.

Notice that the equipping gifts were not part of the list of "presentations by the Spirit," or the list in Romans. They're given by the Lord to help equip all the saints to minister, whereas these other gifts are given to bring all together.

Any gift can be used outside a meeting, but "a presentation given to each person by the Spirit," is Body-meeting specific. How happy the Head must be to finally be able to use His whole Body!

In 1Corinthians 12 Paul lists gifts again:

1Cor 12:27-31, 14:1 (literal translation): Now you are Christ's body, and individually members of it. And God has appointed in the [Legislature], first <u>apostles</u>, second <u>prophets</u>, third <u>teachers</u>, then <u>miracles</u>, then <u>gifts of healings</u>, <u>helps</u> [lit., "those who lay hold of"— evangelists?], <u>administrations</u> [lit., "those who steer"— shepherd?], <u>various kinds of tongues</u>. Not all [are] apostles, not all [are] prophets, not all [are] teachers, not all [work] miracles, not all have gifts of healings, all do not speak with languages, not all <u>interpret</u>. But zealously desire [better] gifts. And yet I show you [how to live] according to a way that's [far exceedingly and abundantly great]. [Next comes chapter 13, about the way of love, then 14:1:] Pursue love, [and] desire earnestly spiritual [things], and more so that you may prophesy.

This list includes both equipping gifts and gifts that we receive and pass on. Paul is telling them that though there is variety in who has or uses which gifts, they should zealously desire "better" gifts. I believe this means, "better" than what one already serves as or uses. We should never become complacent and comfortable with what we've been entrusted with; we should always zealously want more. This is not to be out of personal ambition or vainglory seeking, but out of a zealous desire to see God's kingdom come more, and to edify the Body more.

We're to be seeking these gifts from God, the Giver, and growing in faith/knowledge of them, which accesses them.

Paul goes on from verse 31 to 14:1, to teach about love, that it's a far greater path than gifts. He concludes by saying we should both seek love and zealously desire gifts to edify each other with.

All of the gifts we covered, and whatever others there are, are to be regularly utilized by and for the Legislature.

Eph 4:16 (NASB): ...*the whole body*...according to the proper *working of each individual part*, causes the growth of the body for the building up of *itself* in love.

Rom 12:6 (NASB): Since we have gifts that differ according to the grace given to us, *each of us* is to exercise them

1 Cor 12:7: A presentation of the Spirit is given *to each one* to bring all together.

1 Pet 4:10 (NKJ): As *each one* has received a gift, minister it to one another, as good stewards of the manifold grace [or "gifts"] of God.

God's "manifold grace" is like a diamond, with many facets. He designed Christianity, including meetings, to include the serving of one another with each gift he gives to each believer. So we can see why we need to return to the New Testament format, which included full participation of disciples in meetings.

The preparation for God's People to each share, "by way of revelation or of knowledge or of prophecy or of teaching," is given in 1Corinthians 14:6. All of God's People can be taught to prepare and then serve the group this way.

Early Christian meetings included room for everyone to speak:

1 Cor 14:26 (NKJ): Whenever you come together, *each of you* has a psalm, has a teaching, has a tongue, has a revelation, an interpretation. Let all things be done for edification.

Rom 12:3-8 (NASB): For through the grace given to me I say to everyone among you not to think more highly of himself than he ought to think; but to think so as to have sound judgment, as God has allotted to *each* a measure of faith.

1 Pet 4:10-11 (NKJ): As *each one* has received a gift, minister it to one another, as good stewards of the manifold grace of God. If *anyone* speaks, let him speak as the oracles of God. If *anyone* ministers, let him do it as with the ability which God supplies, that in all things God may be glorified through Jesus Christ, to whom belong the glory and the dominion forever and ever. Amen.

In a large meeting, because of time constraints, this will be best done among smaller, broken-up groups, but all share. Paul told everyone to "desire earnestly to prophesy" in the meeting (1Cor 14:39), and he described a time when everyone in attendance prophesies:

1 Cor 14:24-25 (NKJ): But if all prophesy, and an unbeliever or an uninformed person comes in, he is convinced by all, he is convicted by all. And thus the secrets of his heart are revealed; and so, falling down on his face, he will worship God and report that God is truly among you.

Paul also said,

1 Cor 14:39-40 (NASB): ...do not forbid to speak in [supernatural languages]. But all things must be done properly and in an orderly manner.

He gave instructions on how to utilize the gifts of "various tongues" and "interpretation of tongues" in an orderly way:

1 Cor 14:27-28 (NASB): If anyone speaks in a tongue, it should be two or at the most three, and each in turn, and one must interpret; but if there is no interpreter, he [the first person] must keep silent in the [meeting of the Legislature]; and let him speak to himself and to God.

In other words, if someone wants to share a message via supernatural languages, he/she can do so, but only if someone can interpret. The speaker should stand with one or two others and their speaking should be by turns, not all at once, and with the supernatural interpretation. But if no one believes they can interpret at that time, no sharing in supernatural languages is permitted. The person can still speak in supernatural languages in the meeting, but not as a public ministry, but "between himself and God" (i.e., in a whisper).

In the next two verses, Paul goes on to share how to publically prophesy in an orderly way:

1 Cor 14:29-33 (NASB): Let two or three prophets speak, and let the others pass judgment. But if a revelation is made to another who is seated, the first one must keep silent. For you can all prophesy one by one, so that all may learn and all may be exhorted; and the spirits of prophets are subject to prophets; for God is not a God of confusion but of peace, as in all the [Legislatures] of the saints.

Again, two or three people should present at a time, for the sake of order. Because of verse 31 ("you can all prophesy"), verse 24, and other verses, I believe Paul is using the term "prophet" to represent whoever is prophesying at the time, the "prophesier," rather than the specific ministry of a prophet. However, at the very least, this format should be available to those with the equipping gift of prophet so that the Body can regularly benefit from God through them.

According to this Scripture, there is to be order, and those prophesying must give preference to one another, including to those sitting. There should be room for everyone to share at any time if a revelation's given. Also, there must be accountability. Those sitting should judge the prophecies. Those presenting can briefly discuss them as well, if profitable. And turns can be taken so that "all can prophecy," and "*all* may learn" to.

Whether the "you can all prophesy" in the verse above is speaking only to prophets or to all disciples, there must be a format for all present to begin to prophesy, to eventually fulfill verse 24: "If all prophesy and an unbeliever or ignorant [believer] walks in…" (see also Ac 2:16-18).

Prophecy is to be judged by the Spirit in each of us (1Jn 2:20-21) and by the Word (2Tim 3:16). All believers are to take part in this, not just one person or a few people *for* a group. We're each to develop spiritual sensitivity over time, "by reason of use," in order to test (Heb 5:14). In other words, you learn to test by testing. If one person always tests for a whole group, the group will remain infants in this area. The control and the babysitting must end.

Another thing that's for sure: if we don't choose to test, for whatever reason, we will eventually be deceived by counterfeits. Paul said to all the believers in Thessalonica,

1 Thes 5:19-22 (NKJ): Do not quench the Spirit. Do not despise prophecies. Test all things; hold fast what is good.

Lastly, beyond the meetings, shepherds should seek to make sure disciples are retaining the good they receive in meetings. The feelings and glory that often accompanies prophecy and other gifts of the Spirit are wonderful, but disciples need to retain the good words they receive, through meditation and application.

I suggest that the platform used to share in this kind of meeting not be too spectacular or traditional. Otherwise, the physical arrangement itself may cause people to over-estimate those who speak in front and keep them from ever stepping up to use the gifts God wants to give them for the group. Big stages are good for performances and great for evangelism and more formal teaching. But to include everyone's gift, we'll need to come down to a common, less intimidating, level plane. Let God and the Truth be great, and the rest of us be servants (which really is great).

From this chapter and Truth covered in earlier chapters, we can see that the main meetings included the following:

1. Prayer, which was to be of first importance
2. A "Love Feast," which included the bread and wine (or juice), and was organized by the servers
3. Scripture reading (1Tim 4:13, 1Thes 5:27, Col 4:16-17, Lk

4:16-17, Rev 1:3)
4. <u>Open sharing</u>, each having a presentation in the meeting, with the help of the Spirit; a variety of gifts being used. Overseers knew to serve *together with others* in the group rather than primarily or exclusively, and they were careful to keep the attention on the Lord, who works through each member. They'd silently watch from the background to ensure everyone was ministering and healthy. They'd diligently follow up outside the meeting if sheep were unaccounted for or seemed hurt
5. <u>Accountability</u>, as Jesus said, if a person who was sinning refused to change after being confronted by several disciples on two occasions, the matter was to be brought before the Legislature. Also, Elders who persist in sin are to be "reproved before everyone" by other leadership, "so that the others may take warning" (1Tim 5:20). All of this accountability, so severely lacking today, must be done "with all gentleness keeping an attentive eye on yourself, lest you should be tempted also" (Gal 6:1)

Furthermore, there were other meetings with specific purposes such as for prayer (sometimes with fasting), for witnessing two by two, for teaching, planning, delivering food to the truly needy (1Tim 5:16), training, laying on of hands, etc. These all had free crossover between all disciples, as they were all known to be in the *same* Legislature, owned only by the One who purchased it with his own blood (Ac 20:28).

How often to meet like this and other specifics are up to leaders to determine.

Through re-implementing all of this, eventually it will be said of us as it was said to the Legislature in Corinth:

1 Cor 1:4-7 (NASB): I thank my God always concerning you for the grace of God which was given you in Christ Jesus, that *in everything* you were enriched in Him, in all *speech* and all *knowledge*, even as the testimony concerning Christ was *confirmed* [among] you, so that you are *not lacking in any gift*, awaiting eagerly the revelation

of our Lord Jesus Christ...

2 Cor 8:7 (NIV): ...you excel in everything—in faith, in speech, in knowledge, in complete earnestness and in your love...

Chapter 34
Money Collection & Allocation

As every member of the Body begins to minister, we need to consider how to receive and distribute financial gifts.

Elders oversee and shepherd, which requires a lot of time and hard work. In Ephesus, a system was put in place for them to be paid for this. Paul said those elders who not only performed eldership duties but also "worked hard in Word" should be paid twice as much since they worked twice as hard (1Tim 5:17-18).

At least some elders in Ephesus also worked physical jobs (Ac 20:33-35). This was not considered less spiritual than those who served God's People full-time. Both are necessary at times. In the original Legislatures, even Christian indentured servants were recognized as royal, and it was known their work would result in eternal inheritance (Col 3:23-24).

It's only reasonable that those benefiting from shepherding and teaching should financially support those working hard for them (see Gal 6:6), once mature enough to know to do so. Those benefiting from the use of a public facility should contribute to the cost of it. These things are reasonable and seem obvious to the mature, but disciples still require God's Word to grow in them over time, before they can do so by faith. Giving should never be forced (2Cor 9:7), but disciples can grow in the grace of giving over time, by faith, according to the Spirit, who is gentle and patient with us (2Cor 8:7).

Who should collect and allocate the money given by those being shepherded and taught? Paul instructed Timothy in regard to how to allocate funds (1Tim 5:3-18). As an apostle, according to 1Thes 1:1 & 2:6, Timothy had administrative responsibility, and he was to instruct the Legislature in Ephesus about fund allocation (1Tim 5:7). Acts records a group of elders dealing with money also (Ac 11:30).

Those in the role of <u>server</u> (Gr., diakonos, often transliterated "deacon"), are appointed by leadership and entrusted with great responsibility. They're in charge of finances in order to purchase food and distribute it at the fellowship meals of the Legislature. They also distribute food to the poor. Like elders, they have to pass a character test, which includes a good reputation and being filled with the Spirit and wisdom (Ac 6:3), among several other qualities (1Tim 3:8-13).

So the public leadership should be involved in the receiving and allocating of funds. It should be regularly allocated to the truly needy among us (see 1Tim 5:4, 16), to the leadership, to the servers, to teachers (Gal 6:6), to evangelists (Mt 10:9-14, 1Cor 9:14) and to others, according to the needs, the work done, and the available funds.

If leaders only pay themselves, they're not doing a good job of allocating.

Most ministering goes unpaid, financially speaking. It will all be rewarded, though, at the resurrection of the righteous (see Lk 14:14). Also much giving should go on outside of meetings, as disciples encounter various needs and opportunities.

When Paul and others were given the task of administering the giving of money from one Legislature to support another, they took great pains to show their work was blameless (see 2Cor 8:20). In light of their example, we can become much more careful about the way we report the use of money. It should be collected and delivered carefully and transparently.

In the case of Legislatures that are still being founded, the apostolic team may do well to not receive any money from the new believers at the very first, so that their Gospel isn't slandered (1Cor 9:12). For the same reason, I believe evangelists should not take money from those they're evangelizing, or ever appear to do so. But ALL believers should learn to give generously and with faith and expectation.

Part 6: Knowing All This, What do I do?

Chapter 35
Submission is Necessary, Cleansing, & Powerful

1 Pet 5:1-3 (NKJ): The elders who are among you I exhort...shepherd the flock of God which is among you, serving as overseers, not by compulsion but willingly, not for dishonest gain but eagerly; nor as being lords over those entrusted to you, but being examples to the flock...

After Peter exhorts elders in this letter, he immediately exhorts those who are being served by them:

1 Pet 5:5 (NKJ): Likewise you younger people, *submit yourselves to your elders...*

Then he addresses everyone:

1 Pet 5:5-6 (NKJ): ...Yes, all of you be submissive to one another, and be clothed with humility, for "God resists the proud, but gives grace to the humble." Therefore humble yourselves under the mighty hand of God, that He may exalt you...

Having said all I have regarding elders, I definitely want to speak to those who are being shepherded by them. It is an essential requirement of God that every believer learn submission to elders, when possible, and to other human authorities. This is part of the narrow path Jesus taught.

Two Greek words for "submit" in the New Testament are "hupotasso" and "hipeiko." The first literally means, "to be arranged/ordered under." This involves ordering your life and conduct under a person's instruction. The second means, "to yield under." This involves yielding rather than holding to one's own desire and understanding. It's required when there is a difference of opinion on what to do in a practical matter.

All believers, and especially younger ones, need their lives ordered according to the ways of the faith. The teaching aspect of the initiation into Christianity, coupled with oversight, is received through submission. The lives of disciples are to be totally reordered, so they can become wineskins fit to hold the Gospel.

The developing of a Christian lifestyle takes time. Doing so often requires submission to overseers and mentors. Paul instructed the believers in Corinth to let their lives be ordered under the command of those who were older and had advanced further in the faith, such as Stephanas:

1 Cor 16:15-16 (NKJ): I urge you, brethren—you know the household of Stephanas, that it is the firstfruits of Achaia [the first to receive the Lord there], and that they have devoted themselves to the ministry of the saints—that you also submit to [Gr., "be arranged/ordered under"] such, and to everyone who works and labors with us.

One of the great benefits of leadership is that it gives people an opportunity to submit, out of fear of God, and to thereby receive grace from God for their life. It enables disciples to go much further than they would've on their own, and it's very cleansing for their souls because of the humility involved. It weeds out rebellion from our souls, creating for us a much more peaceful life and walk with the Lord. If we can submit to a human in view of the invisible God—even if we really think we're right, or even if we are right on a non-essential issue—we will be able to submit to the Holy Spirit. It helps us learn to not rely on our own understanding. This, in turn, will help us learn to give up our own understanding for the leading of the Holy Spirit. It's great training, and it's a test.

Submissions to parents, husbands, employers, national governments, and each other as believers are other great opportunities to demonstrate pure fear of God, trust in God, and submission to him. These are all very cleansing and open the way for grace. If the character of a person in authority (e.g., a human king) doesn't represent God well, submitting anyway based on God's appointing of that office is very cleansing. It makes God's People shine. They can see God—not just the human involved.

If a person in authority goes so far as to command disobedience to God, in that area "we must obey God rather than men" (Ac 5:27-29). This is also out of the fear of God. However, even in such tragic cases, we are to respect the office God created and stay submissive in heart, as David did toward King Saul when Saul was out of control. This having to obey God rather than human authority is also a test, on the other end of the spectrum. God wants us to always keep Jesus as our highest authority (i.e., "Lord").

Let's look again at submission to God-appointed elders:

Heb 13:17 (NKJ): Obey those who [Gr., "lead"] you, and be submissive ["yield under them"], for they watch out for your souls, as those who must give account. Let them do so with joy and not with grief, for that would be unprofitable for you.

Jesus actually entrusts his People's souls into the care of human elders. This makes their job very serious and powerful. There is a solemn authority there, given with this trust. I've recommended elders get more involved in believers' lives than the Roman Catholic/Protestant leadership model teaches. If and as they do, their spiritual authority and power to oversee and shepherd believers will become evident in many cases. Believers must choose in themselves to yield under their instruction in order to benefit from their function in the Body.

Believers need elders. Though there are not multiple

Legislatures (ekklesia) in your city, but only one, there may be many elderships, vested with authority from heaven. We must solemnly respect them, highly esteem them, and, when possible, utilize their ministries.

1 Thes 5:12-13 (NKJ): And we urge you, brethren, to recognize those who labor among you, and [stand before] you in the Lord and admonish you, and to esteem them very highly in love for their work's sake.

By yielding, we exercise the Lamb nature, which releases the Power of God. This is one reason apostles and other traveling servants like to join with and submit to local leaders when in a city ministering to God's People. They want the grace and power from God that comes through submission to others. Also, such humility helps them make fewer mistakes.

We all have areas of our minds & souls that are not renewed yet, blind spots, areas of darkness and hardness. Though the Lord by the Spirit may be speaking to us internally, because of the condition of our souls we may not acknowledge him and obey. So we need each other. We need his input through other believers who have a different perspective than our own. Plus, I've observed that sometimes he chooses *only* to speak to us through others.

We've all heard of great, gifted men/women of God who did great miracles and later fell. Often in these cases, the help God sent them to keep them from falling was through people in their lives. But they didn't humble themselves to listen to these people. Had they done so, they would've received the grace they needed from God to continue on well. So staying submissive is staying under the protection of humility, where we can access God's grace.

Mature believers will not need as much oversight and ordering of their lives by elders. Elders need to feel out and determine how much they should do for different people. They by no means need to do every aspect of shepherding for every believer they come in contact with. They'd burn out trying! Their shepherding is to help believers learn to be shepherded by the Lord himself, for the rest of their lives. Over time, the person is to mature and need less and less human shepherding.

This being said, in *all* cases believers need to be submissive to each other. Elders need to be submissive to each other and even to younger believers, to a degree. It's all a humility test. Younger believers will need to submit to elders more often, of course. Older believers who are not elders in the city also need to maintain an attitude of submissiveness toward elders, even if they don't need much oversight, and toward everyone else. We're commanded, "All of you be submissive to one another" (1Pe 5:5).

Chapter 36
We're Free to Serve Humbly in Love

Gal 5:13 (NIV): You, my brothers and sisters, were called to be free. But do not use your freedom [as an opportunity for] the flesh; rather, serve one another humbly in love.

1 Pet 2:16-17 (NASB): [Live] as free men, and do not use your freedom as a covering for evil, but as bondslaves of God. Honor all people, love the brotherhood...

    This book is a call for reformation, *not* a revolution. Revolutions are bloody. They involve the overthrow of current leaders in order to radically change societies. This is not acceptable to God for us. We're to lead by example and speak the truth in love. When the religious people of Jesus' day killed him, he forgave and died for them. Their attacks are always stepping stones to defeat Satan and bring more freedom to people, including some of them. We *have to* "overcome evil with good" (Rom 12:21).
    I hope that through this book you've been able to align your vision with truth more. Now I want to share several keys that will help us keep advancing on the narrow path. The first is *that we don't stop with knowledge, but stay humble and choose to love.* The truths that really help our lives come from above. We can access them through being like children. Take a look at what Jesus said here:

Luke 10:21 (NKJ): In that hour Jesus rejoiced in the Spirit

and said, "I thank You, Father, Lord of heaven and earth, that You have hidden these things from the wise and prudent and revealed them to babes. Even so, Father, for so it seemed good in Your sight."

Scripture also says:

1 Cor 8:1-3 (NKJ): ...We know that we all have knowledge. Knowledge puffs up, but love edifies. And if anyone thinks that he knows anything, he knows nothing yet as he ought to know. But if anyone loves God, this one is known by Him.

I think the danger in learning things from God is that we become proud of our knowledge. But what really makes us special is the death of Jesus the King in our place.

No matter how much knowledge or anything else we've received from God, we always have to remember that we can't credit ourselves for having received it:

1 Cor 4:7 (NKJ): For who makes you differ from another? And what do you have that you did not receive? Now if you did indeed receive it, why do you boast as if you had not received it?

We can only be thankful. Next Paul goes on to say, sarcastically and painfully,

1 Cor 4:8 (NKJ): You are already full! You are already rich! You have reigned as kings without us—and indeed I could wish you did reign, that we also might reign with you!

The Lord Jesus shared the same frustration with another Legislature. He said to the disciples in Laodicea:

Rev 3:17-18 (NKJ): ...you say, 'I am rich, have become wealthy, and have need of nothing'—and do not know that you are wretched, miserable, poor, blind, and naked—I

counsel you to buy from Me gold refined in the fire, that you may be rich; and white garments, that you may be clothed, that the shame of your nakedness may not be revealed; and anoint your eyes with eye salve, that you may see.

We all have to be very careful not to receive some of the good God intends for us, get proud of that, and thereby stop short of all the good God wants for us.

Phil 3:12-15 (NKJ): Not that I have already attained, or am already perfected; but I press on, that I may lay hold of that for which Christ Jesus has also laid hold of me. Brethren, I do not count myself to have apprehended; but one thing I do, forgetting those things which are behind and reaching forward to those things which are ahead, I press toward the goal for the prize of the upward call of God in Christ Jesus. Therefore let us, as many as are mature, have this [mindset].

My goal is that you receive truth from this book that will set you free in various areas—free to love more and serve more. As you're getting free, there may be a temptation to look down on others. But doing that is not consistent with freedom:

1 Pet 2:16-17 (NIV): Live as free men, but do not use your freedom as a cover-up for evil; live as servants of God. Show proper respect to everyone: Love the brotherhood of believers...

I imagine this book has downloaded some wisdom on you. There's a humility that goes with wisdom that we need to strive to maintain:

James 3:13, 17-18 (NIV): Who is wise and understanding among you? Let him show it by his good life, by deeds done in the humility that comes from wisdom...the wisdom that comes from heaven is first of all pure; then

peace-loving, considerate, submissive, full of mercy and good fruit, impartial and sincere. Peacemakers who sow in peace raise a harvest of righteousness.

The truth about all of us is that, "we know in part…" (1Cor 13:9), and even if we did "understand all mysteries and all knowledge," without love, we would be "nothing" (1Cor 13:2).

1 Cor 13:4-7 (NKJ): Love [is patient] and is kind; love does not envy; love does not parade itself, is not puffed up; does not behave rudely, does not seek its own, is not provoked, thinks no evil; does not rejoice in iniquity, but rejoices in the truth; bears all things, believes all things, hopes all things, endures all things.

Moving on, the second key is that when it comes to reformation, *the first place we need to start is with ourselves, rather than with others, and we need to be merciful instead of judgmental.* Our focus, in terms of correction, has to be on our own problems rather than those of others:

Matt 7:3-5 (NKJ): And why do you look at the speck in your brother's eye, but do not consider the plank in your own eye? Or how can you say to your brother, "Let me remove the speck from your eye"; and look, a plank is in your own eye? Hypocrite! First remove the plank from your own eye, and then you will see clearly to remove the speck out of your brother's eye.

This is not easy at times, but it's something we all have to do. If we don't, or I could say *when* we don't, our brother's problems are maximized in our eyes and we become blind to our own problems. We want so badly to fix our brother or sister, but we're disabling ourselves from helping him or her by not fixing ourselves. And, then, we aren't able to fix ourselves either. But if we choose to see our own problems, we'll be able to get help from the Lord for them, and then through him we'll be able to help others. This is a discipline to keep working on for sure.

If we judge others, focusing too much on their faults, we will end up doing the same things and being judged by God for them:

Matt 7:1-2 (NKJ): Judge not, that you be not judged. For with what judgment you judge, you will be judged; and with the measure you use, it will be measured back to you.

Rom 2:1 (NASB): ...you have no excuse, everyone of you who passes judgment, for in that which you judge another, you condemn yourself; for you who judge practice the same things.

Then, we can't escape God's judgment ourselves:

Rom 2:2-4 (NASB): And we know that the judgment of God rightly falls upon those who practice such things. But do you suppose this, O man, when you pass judgment on those who practice such things and do the same yourself that you will escape the judgment of God? Or do you think lightly of the riches of His kindness and tolerance and patience, not knowing that the kindness of God leads you to repentance?

God is rich in kindness, tolerance, and patience—with everyone. So we have to see others through those lenses and be the same way toward them. God helped us change our thinking because he's kind, tolerant, and patient, so how can we turn around and not be that way toward others who need change?

Rom 14:10, 12-13 (NKJ): But why do you judge your brother? Or why do you show contempt for your brother? For we shall all stand before the judgment seat of Christ...each of us shall give account of himself to God. Therefore let us not judge one another anymore...

Rather than judging, we can do something else. Since we're

all going to make mistakes, the best investment for our future is to give mercy to people:

Matt 5:7 (NKJ): Blessed are the merciful, for they shall obtain mercy.

James 2:13 (NKJ): ...judgment is without mercy to the one who has shown no mercy. Mercy triumphs over judgment.

Judgment in our heart results in criticism coming out of our mouths. So the third key is to *not speak evil of each other, but be part of the solution, by intercession.* We need to guard our heart and our tongues:

James 4:11-12 (NKJ): Do not speak evil of one another, brethren. He who speaks evil of a brother and judges his brother, speaks evil of the law and judges the law. But if you judge the law, you are not a doer of the law but a judge. There is one Lawgiver, who is able to save and to destroy. Who are you to judge another?

James 5:9 (NKJ): Do not grumble against one another, brethren, lest you be condemned. Behold, the Judge is standing at the door!

Rather than criticizing, we should *intercede*. This is an extremely powerful expression of love, a weapon in our arsenal we don't want to neglect:

1 Pet 4:8 (NKJ): And above all things have fervent love for one another, for "love will cover a multitude of sins."

We cover people's sins against us, before God, by choosing to forgive them out of love.

To summarize, the three keys I've shared are:

1. Rather than becoming proud of our knowledge, choose to stay humble and serve out of love

2. Focus on ourselves to change first and foremost, and show mercy rather than judging
3. Guard our mouths from criticizing, and instead intercede

God set life up such that new generations benefit from preceding ones and can therefore go further than them. This is true in regard to physical possessions, knowledge, technology, etc., and of spiritual things. My generation naturally takes for granted the spiritual knowledge and understanding that the one before us struggled to obtain. My generation started out better off than the last in some ways, so it's natural we advance further. We'd better! This is God's plan. The challenge each generation faces is to recognize and appreciate the previous generation of soldiers, and continue to receive from them, despite having advanced further in some areas. If it wasn't for the first, the second couldn't have gone further.

Also by covering the sins of the previous generation through forgiveness, mercy, and intercession, we help keep ourselves from falling into the same traps they fell into. And if we can stay thankful and honor our spiritual forefathers as we proceed, it will bring them joy and result in great blessing for us and those who come after us.

Chapter 37
Look up to Jesus

Now I want to give some general advice on how to implement the reforms I've called us to in this book. I'll address all disciples first and then leaders specifically. Our overall responsibility, as always, is to follow the way of love (1Cor 14:1), stay in the light of the Truth (1Jn 1:7), and be led by the Holy Spirit (Rom 8:14). It's hard to know what to do sometimes. However, we've been given a great truth to encourage us: "Love never fails" (1Cor 13:8).

What I recommend you do first of all is to stay free in your direct connection to the Head and in your view of fellow believers. No matter what hierarchies men set up, see all believers as on the same plane. Otherwise, the enemy will take advantage of you through those who place themselves (or allow themselves to be placed) on a higher hierarchical level than you. They don't realize what they're doing, so don't blame them. But *keep yourself free!* You have a ministry to do which only you can do, and which you must do. Jesus is your primary Shepherd, and even he considered himself one of the sheep (Isa 53:7, Jn 1:29) and was crucified in serving us. So if anyone puts himself above you the way the world's leaders do, rather than simply serving you, don't come under him or her. Stay on a level plane with the person, even if it means leaving a hierarchical system (while attempting to remain united in Spirit under the one Head, Jesus).[28]

---

[28] Scripture speaks of "over-seers" as being *"among* you" (1Pe 5:1-2); they

If you find yourself in bondage through one of these systems, you need to respectfully excuse yourself. If any man claims exclusivity of right to minister to you, or if you fear being ex-communicated or lost apart from a human organization, get outta there now!!! Rather than a hierarchical system that gains the approval of men, you need the five activities listed in Acts 2, which I described in this book. You'll certainly need people: humble, faithful leaders God appoints in your town or city, examples, teachers, companions, co-laborers, and a variety of many others. You *will need* human organizations at times—don't get me wrong. However, the first and foremost thing you need is the Lord Jesus. You need a clear and direct connection with him. Let no one get between you and him.

God *does* give men spiritual authority, as we've covered in this book, and you want to utilize that authority. That will sometimes mean being part of human organizations. What you want is the organization to be formed around God-given authority, which it often is. We must network, be in relationship with, and fellowship with God's People, so we will often need to utilize organizations. However, we're never to worship or exalt organizations, or to view them as more than what they actually are. The Legislature is much bigger than any human organization. Within it are many ministries, networks, and relationships.

If a leader crosses the line and begins to attempt to run your life by their mind, rather than the Spirit and the Word, my advice is to respectfully push him/her back and keep working with that person. If he persists in not allowing you to be led by the Spirit, whether knowingly or subconsciously, stay clear of that person.

I recommend learning to discern and respond to spiritual authority that God shows you in people. You can ask with faith for him to help you see it, and he will. Also, be careful to maintain an attitude of respect and humility toward all of God's People.

---

watch over you while still among you. Also they're not to exercise authority over us the way the world does (Mt 20:25-28, Lk 22:25-27, 2Cor 1:24).

I recommend you go through the initiation process into Christianity I described in Chapters 18 and 19, if you haven't already. The five equipping gifts listed in Ephesians 4:11 are given by the Lord to take you through it. If you don't have access to this help where you live, the Lord can give part of it to you nowadays through books, videos, and audio messages. You can't receive shepherding through books, but you can pray for it. It's possible you may need to rely only on Jesus for your personal shepherding, since this ministry is still so rare now. But if you ask, he may send you the help you need through shepherds, even if they don't know their ministry by name. You have to keep your eyes open.

If you persist to make it through the equipping you need, you'll be increasingly suitable for service in the Kingdom. You'll be fully prepared "for works of ministry" (Eph 4:11-12, 2Tim 2:20-21, 3:16). He'll use you to help others grow and mature.

I also recommend you use those five "original Christian activities" as a gauge. If you're missing one, work on adding it to your life. Step out—don't be afraid to step out and make changes. The Spirit will lead you as he sees you stepping out according to God's Word. Obviously, you may not be able to participate in all of them right away, or maintain them all at all times, but pray and look for opportunities. If there's nothing for you to join, the Lord may use you to start something yourself.

It is essential that we do our best to stay involved with other disciples, whether regularly attending a traditional meeting or not (2Tim 2:22, Heb 10:24-25). The many "one-anothers" of Scripture are commands to us (see list in Chapter 28). We've got to position ourselves to obey them, even if it means tolerating various aspects of tradition. I've found the benefits of Jesus' presence and power, through gathering into Jesus authority (Mt.18:20), far outweigh the personal inconvenience involved.

You also must fulfill your ministry. This is a responsibility, and you and I will be judged by the Lord based on it (Mt 25:14-30). As you position yourself around other, growing disciples in the context of "serving one another in love," and/or doing outreach, you'll naturally utilize and discover your ministry-gift(s) as well as gifts of the Spirit to serve effectively.

As you put Jesus first and seek a full Christian lifestyle, you will go against the grain of many people around you. The enemy will try to stop you through accusation, which will likely come through friends at times. Intimidation may come out of people's mouths. People may list the reasons they stopped advancing, to keep you from advancing on your journey toward more of what God intends for you. Don't be concerned with that. Just commit before the Lord himself to fulfilling his calling for your life, no matter where it takes you. He'll never leave you nor forsake you. And if you get rejected out of a religious system, Jesus will meet you out there and give you the help you need (see Jn 9:35).

Joseph went through such a trial, betrayed by his own brothers, cast out from among them. Because he kept his eyes on God and his plan, and kept from turning bitter or vengeful, eventually he was used to feed a multitude of people who would've otherwise died through famine. Among them were the same brothers who'd earlier betrayed him. "What man meant for evil, God meant for good" (Gen 50:20).

Personally, what's worked for me is to utilize the traditional form of Christianity to the extent that it is needed and spiritually profitable, providing one or more of the "original Christian activities" listed in Acts 2. While doing that, I keep myself free from coming under the power of hierarchical tradition and legalism, and I recognize my membership in the whole Legislature in my city. Staying free *and* involved is sometimes not easy, but it *can* often be done. However, there are definitely times when I must take breaks from the traditional form, or periods when I leave it completely. Regardless of that, I do my best to stay involved with other disciples and in fulfilling Great Commission.

I also have to continue to apply Biblical truth to my own mind regarding our identity as believers, as Kings and Priests, as part of the *one* Legislature in our city, as being directly under Jesus the Head, etc. I find my legitimacy in being *"in Him"* rather than in human organizations. From that standpoint, I seek to edify the Body any way I can, build strong connections with individuals as well as I can, and work with anyone working to complete the Great Commission.

Regarding leaders, equippers and public speakers you come across, I recommend you ask God for the ability to recognize their gifts. You want to know what function(s) they have when possible and utilize their services if they are speaking the truth in love. "Test all things; hold on to the good" (1Thes 5:21). Love and intercede for them when you discover problems. "Be wise as serpents and innocent as doves" (Mt 10:16).

Also, it is very important not to try to uproot false ministers. As Jesus said, we are to protect our minds from hypocritical teachings that come from self-exalted people (Lk 12:1). Paul said to "turn away" from those "having a form of godliness but denying its power" (2Tim 3:5). So, on the one hand, we *must* protect ourselves, and we should protect those around us as much as we can. We also shouldn't worry about the truth offending some people:

Matt 15:12-14 (NASB): ...the disciples [said] to Him, "Do You know that the Pharisees were offended when they heard this statement?" But He answered and said, "Every plant which My heavenly Father did not plant shall be uprooted. Let them alone; they are blind guides of the blind. And if a blind man guides a blind man, both will fall into a pit."

However, on the other hand, *we* aren't called to uproot false teachers, false prophets, false apostles, etc. That's not our responsibility and would cause more harm than good; it will be the job of angels at the end of the age:

Matt 13:24-30 (NKJ) (interpretation from Matt 13:36-42 inserted in brackets): ...The kingdom of heaven is like a man [the Son of Man] who sowed good seed [the sons of the Kingdom] in his field [the world]; but while men slept, his enemy [the devil] came and sowed tares [the sons of the wicked one] among the wheat and went his way. But when the grain had sprouted and produced a crop, then the tares also appeared. So the servants [true believers] of

the owner came and said to him, "Sir, did you not sow good seed in your field? How then does it have tares?" He said to them, "An enemy has done this." The servants said to him, "Do you want us then to go and gather them up?" But he said, "No, lest while you gather up the tares you also uproot the wheat with them. Let both grow together until the harvest [the end of the age], and at the time of harvest I will say to the reapers [the angels], 'First gather together the tares and bind them in bundles to burn them [in the furnace of fire], but gather the wheat into my barn.'"

We can and should warn those around us who we're responsible for of false leaders, who we'll recognize by their fruit. There is also a place for disciplining them, but there's a proper order of who's to confront and reprove, and how to do it (see Tit 1:9-13, 3Jn 10, Gal 5:10, 1Tim 1:20).

In general, I'd say the best way to deal with counterfeits is to be genuine ourselves, and God's supernatural attestation of our lives and message will prove them wrong. If they persist, this attestation may provoke them to crucify us out of envy, exposing what they're really like in front of everyone. Forgiving them as we go down will give an opportunity for many, including some of them, to recognize truth, come to their senses, and change their thinking and life. God also may publically discipline them, maybe even through us, by the Holy Spirit. But to be right, we have to maintain the lamb nature.

If you are a leader in Christianity, first I suggest you determine, before God, the source of your authority. Jesus was "the Root and the Offspring of [King] David" (Rev 22:16). If Jesus is not the root of our ministries—if we don't proceed out from him—our offspring won't be of him either. We'll be wasting our time. We won't bear lasting fruit. Even worse, we'll be counterfeits of the real thing, and we'll miss our true calling.

If you're a true leader in your city, and you've been ministering according to the Catholic/Protestant pattern, I obviously suggest you make the adjustments called for in this book. If you are involved in providing traditional meetings for

God's People, and you occupy the traditional pastor position in the structure, I suggest you lower yourself (or lift everyone else up, whichever way you want to look at it) by reforming the system. The whole structure should change, and these changes need to be made carefully, accompanied by teaching along the way. This will allow people to adapt to changes with faith and understanding. Make room for the Head and all of his Body. Do your ministry always alongside others doing theirs or training to do theirs. Let's all grow up together.

If you're an elder or group of elders and you're involved in providing meetings for God's People, good will increase as you expand what's provide for them. You will have to fight spiritual opposition as you advance, but, eventually, you'll enjoy more good from God. At a certain point, you may notice the enemy change his tactic from resisting you head-on to pushing you from behind. In other words, watch out for pride and boasting among the group, and in yourself of course, based on comparisons with "less advanced" groups. You can get rid of it by teaching on our unity and our end goal, which we're all far from attaining.

Chapter 38
Questions & Answers

The following questions were contributed by a few friends:

1. How can we bring about this "Jesus-Church" (not man-owned or controlled)?

Basically, it will take the Head to bring it about, along with our cooperation. I was called by God to help restore some of these lost truths. Others are doing the same. As they become common knowledge among us, we will all be able to act on them and, as a result, become more and more like Jesus' original Legislature. We are part of it already—any of us who have sincere faith in the King—but there's much more we can access of its benefits.

Societal pressures will continue to force us to find God's solutions, written for us in his Word. As pressures continue to increase, the need for change may become more evident to most of us. But I believe that God's plan is to prepare us before storms hit, so he sends his word to us beforehand in a form such as this book.

2. You mentioned that we should encourage each other to teach and listeners should exercise their spiritual discernment. I understand that it's good for each one of us to share and teach. But what can we do to ensure "quality control" of what would be taught? How can we deal with possible confusion due to different teachings on

a subject?

There are several things that will help us with this. The first and foremost of them, I'd say, is a high esteem for the truth in God's Word, the Bible. We each need to develop "the love of the truth" (2Thes 2:10) in order to not be deceived. If we all look highly up to God's Word and have enough humility and love for the truth to not be contentious over it, our teaching will be protected.

The next need is for good teaching ministries. As they operate, they spread a kind of canopy of light over all who listen. This allows people to live according to truth and speak the truth. I think this influence is why teachers will receive stricter judgment (Jas 3:1). If teachers and others provide an example of humility and love for truth, it will also be followed by others.

If some leave the light but still hang around believers as wolves in sheep's clothing, their teaching will be harmful. When it is, typically at least some believers in each meeting will speak up against it. Elders and other mature believers will be able to do this pretty naturally. In this way, the goal of "speaking the truth in love" (Eph 4:15) will be maintained.

Thankfully, in many countries all disciples have Bibles. And all disciples have the Holy Spirit, so that "we all know the truth" (1Jn 2:20). If something is clearly out of line with Scripture, we can show it and all agree. This will work as long as people are willing to change their thinking, which is a foundational requirement of all of us (Heb 6:1). If someone is not, there's a deeper problem. If it's on a major issue, it must eventually be confronted. If it's a minor one, I suggest intercession. We will need to learn to "major on majors and minor on minors," and to put contention to death.

In our meetings, especially those with full participation, we need to become accustomed to seeking the mind of Christ, who's in our midst. We seek it collectively, as a group. Doing this will give us a sensitivity vertically toward him and horizontally toward each other. Then what the Head wants will get done, and the enemy's voice will be minimized.

We all make mistakes, especially in what we say, so there has to be a high tolerance of each other. People need to be allowed to speak, even if they're making a mess of things or making themselves look bad. We're all going to do this at times. Patience with each other while helping steer each other in the right direction is essential if we're going to grow and improve.

Lastly, as apostles and elders are appointed and begin providing oversight more, they will be a powerful force against the more dangerous false teachers and false doctrines, which none of us should tolerate. We should speak up against them, and if we can't change them, stay away from them (Rom 16:17).

3. Isn't your view a radical equalitarian one? Isn't it true in Scripture that someone in leadership always took initiative? Has this way you describe ever worked historically in any serious, long term way?

I documented what I wrote in this book from the Bible, so I can't really call it my view. I'd say that since God's thoughts and ways are higher than ours, his Word would seem radical to us humans. But we're called to lay aside our earthly thinking and take on his thinking. I'm happy I've done that somewhat, and I will need to continue to.

Is this view equalitarian, meaning that all people are equal? Yes. I think it's obvious that Jesus lived and worked this way. He didn't respect the self-promotion of man into roles and titles God didn't create. He himself, the greatest leader, was raised as a carpenter, not a king in a human government. In some ways, that kind of position is way too low for him. He didn't have to be called "chief priest," or be the ruler of a synagogue, big or small. His goal was the Father's will. He chose disciples and apostles from a diverse range of society. They were society's rejects in some cases. Most weren't important figures in the eyes of religious or political society—before or after he trained them. These were the kind of people he felt could be good wineskins to pour the New Covenant Spirit into, if they endured with him.

He told them they're all brothers and taught them that true

greatness had to do with serving. And he sent them a Guide from Heaven to lead in the completion of his Great Commission. This kind of leadership was new on Earth and *very* special.

In Acts, the way the new community of disciples lived was, therefore, very different than any other society or community, totally different. I've heard that the founder of Communism commented on the way this community in Acts lived saying it was the best example of communism ever witnessed on Earth. What he missed is the Holy Spirit. No human government or society can reproduce what appeared on the Earth at that time. How long it lasted is not important. What's important is that it did and can exist, and should exist.

This new kind of society, Jesus' Legislature (ekklesia), was a loosely organized organism. It relied on the Holy Spirit. It was connected together as a literal body—the Body of the resurrected King Jesus. As such, there was an equality of value. No part could say, "I don't need you" to any other. And all were equally under the one Head. This is what Paul meant in 1Corinthians 12:5, "there are varieties of ministries, and the same Lord." Then he went on to show the diversity of each body part, all under the one Head. Each different body part has a unique ministry and all of these are equal in importance, though unique in function.

There *was* a leadership structure, as I documented in this book. There was order. But all were seen and known as kings and priests, and the leaders' job was to ensure the people come to know and act on this, not to do everything.

Lastly, it's *not* true that in Scripture someone in leadership always took initiative. One example is Gideon (Judges 6-8). He was not a leader. He was a weakling. God came to him to show himself strong through a weak vessel. This is more the pattern we see in Scripture. Without God, this kind of leadership could not exist. It's interesting that after God used Gideon so powerfully, the people came to him and asked him to rule over them. "But Gideon said to them, 'I will not rule over you, nor shall my son rule over you; the LORD shall rule over you'" (Judges 8:23). At that time he had the right picture.

David is another example of this, chosen by God as a child—not as a leader. Samuel was too. Moses wasn't fit for spiritual leadership in God's eyes until he'd lost all his apparent qualifications. Peter spoke the first public Gospel message, taking a step of leadership after any possibility of him being a leader among the disciples was broken. Even then, it wasn't he who took the initiative; he was led by the Spirit. Later, among other apostles and elders, when a question came up Peter was among the last to speak up and share his thoughts (Ac 15:7). The Holy Spirit was relied on by the leaders involved.

So what God's calling for in his Word is spiritual. It really requires maintaining an equal view of each other, submissiveness to leadership, and taking action with the help of the Spirit.

Chapter 39
For Leadership without Limits

(Chapter added April, 2020)

God is intent on growing his People up. To keep order and effectively do so, he needs good leaders and equippers. There are clearly two distinct groups among God's People: leaders and non-leaders, as we see in the following verses.

Ps 107:32 (NASB) Let them extol Him also in the congregation of <u>the people</u>, and praise Him at the seat of <u>the elders</u>.

Phil 1:1 (NIV) Paul and Timothy, servants of Christ Jesus, to all <u>God's holy people</u> in Christ Jesus at Philippi, together with the <u>overseers and deacons</u> [assistants to the overseers].

Acts 15:4 (NKJ) And when they had come to Jerusalem, they were received by the <u>church and the apostles and the elders</u>...

Acts 15:22-23 (NKJ) Then it pleased <u>the apostles and elders, with the whole church</u>, to send chosen men of their own company to Antioch with Paul and Barnabas, [namely], Judas who was also named Barsabas, and Silas, leading men among the brethren. They wrote this [letter] by them: <u>The apostles, the elders, and the brethren</u>, To the brethren who are of the Gentiles in Antioch....

This is a true, Scriptural distinction. That said, God's goal was never for leaders to be perpetually observed and the people to perpetually observe. That is a description of the traditional, clergy-laity arrangement. God wants all of His children to grow into maturity, to be led by the Holy Spirit, to be equipped for their works of service. This doesn't mean all become leaders. Leaders set an example and oversee.

> Leader does not = minister
> All disciples = ministers
> Leader = overseer

In the process of growth into leadership, a person will receive faith and abilities they can use to serve God's people with. It could be that *all* leaders are equipping gifts of one kind or another. So they have a ministry to use in equipping others. This is part of their work. The other part, as an overseer, is to watch others serve.

Some leaders *want* the adoration, the admiration, and the glory of a captive audience. Others want God's People to grow into full stature. For that, the People must do works of ministry. This is not in the traditional way, but in their own lives and in full participation meetings and in outreaches.

Passive observers have dead faith. There is no fruit in that for anyone.

For leadership without limits, leaders will need to take the oversight approach, seeking to make those they serve successful in their appointed works. This was how Jesus led his disciples.

I believe that leaders who follow Jesus' example are the greatest force on the earth. They enable the greatest Force to arise. They make the enemy tremble.

You may ask, "So do I have a church or a ministry?" And you may be concerned that these truths are taking your church away from you." Here's my response: You have a Kingdom (Lk 22:29). There are no "churches" as we've thought. There are Legislatures of the Kingdom of God, which are made up of each disciple in each city. They are owned by the Lord only. As a leader, you have a sphere of influence within the Lord's

Legislature on the earth. This is all you need. It allows you to be "a servant of the Legislature" (Ro 16:1) in various places.

2 Cor 10:13 (NASB) But we will not boast beyond [our] measure, but within the measure of the sphere which God apportioned to us as a measure, to reach even as far as you.

1 Cor 9:2 (NASB) If to others I am not an apostle, at least I am to you; for you are the seal of my apostleship in the Lord.

Your servanthood, even in your sphere, is not exclusive to you. And the sheep are not yours.

1Cor 3:5, 21-23 (NASB) What then is Apollos? And what is Paul? Servants through whom you believed, even as the Lord gave [opportunity] to each one. ... So then let no one boast in men. For all things belong to you, whether Paul or Apollos or Cephas or the world or life or death or things present or things to come; all things belong to you, and you belong to Christ; and Christ belongs to God.

Your job, as a leader, is to watch over, warn, protect, facilitate, teach; and it's their job to listen and choose to obey, to follow you, and to grow.

Territorialism on the part of leaders is a problem in the Lord's legislature. The root of this territorialism is possessiveness. You believe a group of Christians are your church. You want to help them and protect them. Give them back to God in your heart; let them go. This will free you and allow him to work more in them. Just serve them and get them to serve others, and the work will multiply. You won't be able to contain it, and the Lord doesn't want you to. It's his Body. He knows how to "nourish and cherish it" (Eph 5:29). You're a Body part; it's your job to just respond to the Head.

Think of yourself as the coach of the Boston Red Sox, a major league baseball team with champion potential. You are not the owner. Nor are you on the field, as far as your coaching role goes. It's your job to make those players shine—in the spotlight, in front of the crowds, they will win the championship.

John the baptizer is a great example of how leadership is supposed to work. He introduced his disciples to the Lamb of God so much so, that when Jesus showed up his disciples left him to follow Jesus. That is success. Train people to be led by the Holy Spirit. Serve them as long as there is opportunity. You may still play a leadership/support role in their lives, for decades. But their heart is to see and follow the Lord more and more, through your services.

I believe that the real key is to follow Jesus' leadership example. Ask him about it and search for it in the Gospels. His first disciples led the same way, so their example is also provided for us.

I devote this chapter to my first father in the faith, R.C. Wedner, who trained me in such a way that there are no limits for me. Without him and all other sincere leaders who have affected my life, I could not have brought this message to you. I know this, and I honor you all. Thank you.

Chapter 40
A Vision of Our Future
(by Derek Prince)

We need to have a vision for our future as we progress toward the end of the age. To help with that, I'm including this excerpt by Derek Prince entitled, "A Glorious Church."[29] I've substituted the word, "Legislature" for "church" in brackets, in accord with what we've covered in this book:

The Scripture says that the [Legislature] for which Jesus will be coming will be a glorious [Legislature]. Yet many people associated with the [Legislature] today have no concept of what this means. The Greek word for *glory* is *doxo*, from which we get the English word *doxology*, meaning "that which ascribes the glory to God."

I came to New Testament Greek by way of classical Greek, and I was a student and teacher of [Greek] philosophy [in which] *doxo* means, "that which seems to be, that which appears..." This definition is very different from the way the word is used in Scripture. While I was studying philosophy, I decided that I would read the gospel of John in Greek. What really puzzled me was John's use of *doxo*. I thought to myself, *How could it be that [Classical Greek] used the word to mean "that which seems to be, that which appears," whereas John used it for "glory"?*

Some years later, when I was wonderfully born again, I suddenly understood the New Testament's use of the word,

---

[29] Derek Prince, *Rediscovering God's Church* (New Kinsington, PA: Whitaker House, 2006), 25; used with permission from Derek Prince Ministries

doxo. The reason for the difference in translation is that God's glory is His presence manifested to man's senses. It is the visible, tangible presence of God; it is that which appears or that which is seen. When I saw this, I realized how the word had come from the meaning of "that which appears" to "glory." The *glory of God* is what appears or is manifested to the senses of man.

Speaking to the Jewish council in Acts 7:2, Stephen said, *"The God of glory appeared to our father Abraham when he was in Mesopotamia."* Abraham knew God by His visible glory. This encounter changed Abraham's life, motives, and ambitions, to the extent that he forsook all to go to the land that God had promised him.

When the Scripture speaks about a glorious [Legislature], therefore, it means a [Legislature] that is filled with the glory of God. It is a [Legislature] that has within it the manifest, visible, tangible, personal presence of almighty God. It does not refer to a [Legislature] that is living on naked faith without any manifestation, but a [Legislature] that has entered into a relationship with God where His visible, personal, tangible presence is with His people.

A [Legislature] that is permeated with the presence of God attracts people. When people sense it, they will say, "What is here? I've never felt anything like this. It's different. What do these people have that I don't?"

That is the glory of God, and it is awesome. When the Glory of God was revealed to Israel, the people bowed with their faces to the ground:

2 Chronicles 7:1-3 (NIV): When Solomon finished praying, fire came down from heaven and consumed the burnt offering and the sacrifices, and the glory of the LORD filled the temple. 2 The priests could not enter the temple of the LORD because the glory of the LORD filled it. 3 When all the Israelites saw the fire coming down and the glory of the LORD above the temple, they knelt on the pavement with their faces to the ground, and they worshiped and gave thanks to the LORD, saying, "He is

good; his love endures forever.

God's presence was so powerful that no one could remain standing. This is the kind of [Legislature] for which Jesus is coming.

Ephesians 5:25-26: Christ...loved the [Legislature] and gave Himself for her, that He might sanctify and cleanse her with the washing of water by the word...

Jesus redeemed the [Legislature] by His blood so that He might sanctify it by the pure water of His word. The blood and the water of the Word are both needed to make the [Legislature] ready for the coming of the Lord. I always honor the blood of Jesus. His blood paid the redemptive price by which we are bought back out of the hand of the devil. Then, after we have been redeemed by the blood, it is the purpose of God that we should be sanctified and cleansed by the washing of the water by the Word. His purpose is clear:

...that He might present her to Himself a glorious [Legislature], not having spot or wrinkle or any such thing, but that she should be holy and without blemish. (verse 27)

Therefore, here are three signs that identify the [Legislature] that Jesus will come for:

1. It is to be glorious.
2. It is to be marked by the manifest presence of God in its midst.
3. It is to be spotless, holy, and without blemish.

...Only through the washing of water by the Word can we become sanctified. I would recommend to you who are leaders that you do something about this. I can remember when, in the [movement I was a part of] in this country (USA), if you got fifty people together for a Bible study, it was a large number of people, but we did take time for the Word. In most [of those] congregations, every Wednesday night was a Bible study night. What has happened to Bible study? In most of the places I go to now, no time is given for Bible study at all. The leaders are responsible both to teach the Bible [or ensure the Bible is taught] and, even more importantly, to teach people how to study the Bible for themselves and to give them a love for the Bible. I feel so sorry for Christians who live on the spiritual equivalent of the kind of diet that is popular today: chips and fast food. There is no fast food in God's kingdom!

...As we acknowledge Christ in all that He is to the [Legislature], we are brought into the unity of the faith, "to a perfect man, to the measure of the stature of the fullness of Christ" [Eph 4:13]. The key word here is *"fullness."* Until the [Legislature] of Jesus Christ demonstrates Christ in all His fullness—in every aspect, every grace, every gift, every ministry—the [Legislature] is not fulfilling its calling. At the present time, we manifest to the world a pathetically small part of the totality of Jesus Christ. There is much of Jesus that the [Legislature] is incapable of demonstrating to the world, but God is going to bring us into that place where the corporate body of Christ will fully reveal the totality of Jesus.

...Paul went on to say,

Ephesians 3:19: ...to know the love of Christ which passes knowledge; that you may be filled with all the fullness of God.

This is a tremendous statement: the [Legislature] of Jesus Christ is going to be the dwelling place of all the fullness of God! The totality of God, in all His nature, in all His power, and in all His aspects, will be manifested in the [Legislature]. There is only one other place in Scripture that I know of where the phrase "the fullness of God" is used, and that is in Colossians 2, where it says of Jesus, *"For in him dwells all the fullness of the Godhead bodily"* (verse 9). In Christ, God was manifested totally, not partially. When the Holy Spirit has completed the work of forming the body of Christ, the fullness of God will be manifested in the [Legislature], as well. Never imagine that this can happen to you alone. You are just a little unit on your own. It is only as you come together into the unity of the faith and the acknowledgment of Christ that you will be able to comprehend with all the believers the width, the length, the depth, and the height, and thus be filled with all the fullness of God. This is the purpose of God for the [Legislature].

The [Legislature] must acknowledge and worship the Lord Jesus Christ. The Scripture says that through faith in Jesus Christ, we are the children of Abraham. (See Galatians 3:7). God said to Abraham, "Your children are going to be like the stars of the sky." (See Genesis 5:15). Normally speaking, when the sun is shining, or even at night, when the moon is shining, we do not pay much attention to the stars. But when the sun has set, and the moon is not shining brightly, and when every natural source of light has been extinguished, the stars shine brighter in the pitch darkness. This is precisely how it is going to be at the close of the age, as darkness covers the earth and deep darkness the people (see Isaiah 60:2); as the night gets darker and darker, the children of Abraham, through faith in Jesus Christ, are going to shine out like the stars in their glory. (See Philippians 2:14-16).

Here is a glimpse of the bride coming forth in her glory:

Song of Solomon 6:10: Who is she who looks forth as the morning, fair as the moon, clear as the sun, awesome as an army with banners?

When the [Legislature] manifests the glory of Christ [her King], the world will recoil in amazement; it never will have seen a [legislature] like this. Who is this coming forth like the morning? After a night of darkness, the [Legislature] will be like the rising of the sun. The bride of Christ will be as beautiful as the moon.

The responsibility of the moon is to reflect the light of the sun, and the moon appears in phases—quarter, half, three-quarter, and full moon. It waxes and wanes, as the [Legislature] of Jesus Christ has waxed and waned. Yet, when the

[Legislature] ultimately comes back to full moon, it will fully reflect the glory of the Son. That is what the world is going to see—a full-orbed [Legislature], completely reflecting the glory and brightness of the Son.

And the [Legislature] will be as clear as the sun. Although it will be as the moon, it will have the righteousness and the authority of the Son of Righteousness, Jesus Christ, applied to it, and it will be as awesome as an army with banners. Who has seen a [Legislature] that is awesome to the forces of evil and darkness, sin and satan? A [Legislature] is coming forth that is going to cause the forces of satan to tremble and flee.

God has shown me through experience that there is one message the devil fears more than any other. It is the message of what the [Legislature] is going to be, and what it is going to do to him. The devil fights against this truth more than any other truth.

This is a picture of the [Legislature] as God intends it to be. Take time to let God challenge you with His plan for the [Legislature] and His plan for your individual life. He is coming back for a glorious [Legislature], and a glorious [Legislature] He will have!

I Have a (Christian) Dream

...that one day God's People will walk with dignity, with shoulders held high, knowing their identity as royal priests in the Kingdom of God.

...that Jesus' People will be recognized by the world for their strength of character, their courage, generosity, uprightness in money matters, distinctiveness in the way they value and live out the covenant of marriage, sacrificial love for one another, and mercy and love for their enemies.

...that the purpose and thrust of Christianity will become the completion of Jesus' Great Commission--proclaiming the Good News and making disciples--and that this purpose will burn hot in the blood of every disciple.

...that the equipping servants will care more about God's People ministering than about their own platform, image before men, or paycheck.

...that elders in each city will unify, recognizing their part in the One Flock in their city, and pray and work together for each sheep's development and safe arrival in Jesus' coming Kingdom.

...that sincere believers will all unify, in heart, in thought, in purpose, and in respect, under the One Head of the Body, Jesus, and lose sight of human organizational or minor doctrinal divisions.

...that what's come to be known as "church" will reform to match the New Testament Scriptures, with freedom and full participation of each member of Jesus' Body, for the full edification of God's People and salvation of the world!

Epilogue: In View of Your Future Harvest

If you have read this far, I'm assuming the Lord has spoken to you through this book. According to the Parable of the Farmer, the truths he illumined for you are now seeds in your heart. What you do with them will determine the amount of blessing that will come out of them for you and for others. Those truths are extremely powerful, and they go against the grain of Satan's kingdom and the world. Because of that, many who read this book will likely lose the truths as soon as they hear them. The traditions and domination of man will "trample it down," and "the birds of the air" will devour it (Lk 8:5), so that no effect will take place.

For those who stand up under the pressure of tradition and "the birds," there will be other tests to pass. These tests are allowed by God for the purpose of refining us, so the words we've received can bear fruit and bring change into the world.

In the second test mentioned, the enemy, because of the word, will bring you tribulation or persecution (Lk 8:13, Mt 13:21). His goal is to scorch and kill the seeds. To prepare for this, you have to let the truths you received take root in your heart—otherwise they won't survive. This requires meditation—mulling over the truths repeatedly in your heart and mind with the help of the Spirit of Truth, believing them, verbalizing them, getting a deep understanding of them (Lk 8:6, Mt 13:23, Mk 4:17).

For this reason, I recommend going through this book *multiple times*, until the seeds in it have taken deep enough root in your heart. Most readers will need to do so, though some who've heard and lived these things may not. Be led by the Spirit regarding this. Once the truths are no longer illumined by God as you read, they've got enough moisture for you to move on (Lk 8:6).

The last test Jesus' mentioned comes through "cares, riches, and pleasures of life"—the weeds (Lk 8:14). These will try to choke out the truths God's put in you. In other words, if we don't live by faith, on the narrow path, embracing choices required of us by God, these seeds won't make any difference in us or the world around us. If we forsake the narrow path, these and other truths will grow dim in our hearts. Choosing to keep walking straight will allow them to grow in our hearts. Passing this third test requires choosing, like Moses did, to lay aside "the riches of Egypt" for that which is eternally lasting. He "chose rather to suffer with the People of God than to enjoy the passing pleasures of sin for a season...because he was looking to the reward" (Heb 11:25-27).

Eventually, having passed these tests, what King Jesus has put in you through this book will bear *major* fruit, "a huge harvest" (Lk 8:15, Living Bible), up to 100 times what was planted in you (Lk 8:8). This will happen through perseverance (vs. 15), but after passing all these tests you'll be accustomed to perseverance. What will matter to you is the harvest. You will have proved yourself a "doer of the word and not merely a hearer" (Jas 1:22). You will have "looked intently" (meditated) and "continued steadfastly" (persevered) in the perfect law of freedom, the Word implanted in you by the Spirit (Jas 1:21). As a result, you, and others with you, "will be blessed in what you do" (Jas 1:25).

A final request: please pray for me and my family. Thank you.

Bibliography & Recommended Resources

The following include good resources I highly recommend for further study.

Recommended, Most Related Resources
- *Pagan Christianity?*, by Frank Viola & George Barna (www.paganchristianity.org). I read Pagan Christianity after completing this book, and I was amazed to see it document from history, all of the major points I documented from Scripture. It's easy to read and very eye-opening. I *highly* recommend it.
- Audio series, by Derek Prince (www.derekprince.org):
    o "The Church—Vol. 1—Universal & Local"
    o "7 Pictures of God's People"
    o "Headship of Jesus"
    o "Witchcraft Exposed and Defeated"
- Video Documentary, "The Last Reformation—The Beginning"

Other Recommended, Works Cited
- Ed Glaspey, Doug Easterday, Linda Frizzell, Jane Akeson, and Dan Wallis. *Restoration School.* Junction City: Restoration Ministries.
- Foxe, John. *Foxe's Christian Martyrs.* Uhrichsville: Barbour Publishing, Inc., 2010.
- Haggard, Ted & Gayle, interview by John Bishop of Living Hope Church. *Ted Haggard Uncensored* Vancouver, WA, (June 19th, 2009).
- Hogan, David (of Freedom Ministries). *Fire of God 1 & 2*. MP3 Audio Messages from 1997-2000.
- Lubben, Shelley. *Truth Behind The Fantasy Of Porn*. USA: Shelley Lubben Communications, 2010.
- Murrow, David. *Why Men Hate Going to Church.* Nashville: Thomas Nelson, Inc., 2005.
- Nettleton, P. Todd. *North Korea: Good News Reaches the Hermit Kingdom.* Bartlesville: Living Sacrifice Book Company, 2008.
- Osborn, TL. *Soul Winning.* OSFO Books International, 1994.
- Platt, David. *Radical.* Colorado Springs: Multnomah Books, 2010.
- Prince, Derek. *Rediscovering God's Church.* New Kinsington:

Whitaker House, 2006.
- Prince, Derek. "Spiritual Warfare." In *On Experiencing God's Power*, 469. New Kensington: Whitaker House, 1998.
- Prince, Derek. "The Church—Vol.1—Universal & Local." (Audio CD#5003). Derek Prince Ministries, 2004.
- Tenney, Tommy. *The God Chasers.* Shippensburg: Destiny Image Publishers, 2001.
- *Transformations: A Documentary.* Directed by The Sentinel Group. 1999.
- "The Persecuted Church Global Report 2011." The Voice of the Martyrs, 2011.
- Wurmbrand, Richard. *Tortured For Christ.* Bartlesville: Living Sacrifice Book Company, 1967. (Free copy currently available from torturedforchrist.com).

Other Works Cited

- Forrester, E.J. *The International Standard Bible Encyclopedia, Vol 1.* Grand Rapids: WM. B. Eerdmans Publishing Co., 1956.
- Seyffert, Oskar. *A Dictionary of Clasical Antiquities.*
- Trench, R.C. *Synonyms of the New Testament.* 7th ed.
- www.britannica.com/EBchecked/topic/177746/Ecclesia.
- www.merriam-webster.com/dictionary/church.
- http://dictionary.reference.com.
- http://en.wikipedia.org/wiki/Shepherd.

www.actschristianity.org